D1029631

REMINISCENCES OF
AN AMERICAN LOYALIST

W.J. .... pinxt.   F. Conat ....

JONATHAN BOUCHER, M.A.

REMINISCENCES OF
AN AMERICAN LOYALIST
1738–1789

Being the *Autobiography* of *The Rev^d*. JONATHAN
BOUCHER, *Rector* of ANNAPOLIS in MARYLAND
and afterwards *Vicar* of EPSOM, SURREY, ENGLAND

EDITED BY HIS GRANDSON
JONATHAN BOUCHIER

With a New Introduction by
Ralph Adams Brown

KENNIKAT PRESS, INC./PORT WASHINGTON, N. Y.

INTRODUCTION TO
THE 1967 REISSUE

JONATHAN BOUCHER was one of the more coherent as well as one of the more verbal of those men and women who supported the Loyalist position during our War for Independence. He was born on March 12, 1738, in the village of Blencogo in Cumberland County, England. His mother operated a small tavern and his father, who appears to have been a ne'er-do-well with some education, sometimes supplemented the family income by teaching school. Boucher was to remember a childhood of privation and poverty.

Inspite of the handicaps, young Boucher appears to have received a better-than-average education. Perhaps because he seemed to be unusually bright, the father and mother tried to make a scholar of him; he began the study of Latin when only six years old. At the age of sixteen he did some teaching in a night school, and then in April, 1759, he sailed for Virginia where he was to be the tutor to the sons of gentlemen at Port Royal.

Boucher was not happy in Virginia and seems to have had a very disdainful attitude toward the intellectual and cultural level of the people he met there. He returned to England in 1762 to prepare for the Anglican clergy, and in 1763 was a clergyman-school master in St. Mary's parish, Caroline County. Among his students was George Washington's step-son, Jacky Custis, and Boucher became well acquainted with the Washington family.

An important turning point in Boucher's career came with his transfer, in 1770, to Saint Anne's parish in Annapolis, Maryland. He soon found Annapolis "the genteelest town in North America" and became actively involved in its social and intellectual life. He came under the influence of the Royal Governor, a man named Eden, and was appointed chaplain to the lower house of the legislature. Boucher himself claims to have exercised a major influence in the shaping of legislation (see page 92), but this influence was apparently considerably less than he was to remember at a later date when writing his memoirs. At least we know that he was unable to prevent the legislature from lowering the salary of the clergy. At any rate, the influence of the Maryland aristocracy and governing class on the Reverend Mr. Boucher was quickly apparent.

Queen Anne's parish in Prince George's County, Maryland, was one of the more desirable Anglican parishes in the entire South. When this became vacant, Governor Eden arranged to have Boucher transferred to it. Sometime in the early 1770's, Jonathan Boucher married a lady named Miss Eleanor Addison. Little is known about her except that she brought a "comfortable dowry" and that shortly after the marriage her husband purchased a plantation on the Potomac.

Throughout the late months of 1774 and the early months of 1775, political tempers were rising. The Reverend Mr. Boucher firmly and vocally espoused the cause of the established order. He refused to accept the direction or even the suggestion of the local committee of safety and preached against its leadership. He was, at least once, prevented from entering his pulpit by a group of armed men, and he tells us that he never preached a sermon without loaded pistols by his side. He became more and more unpopular and was burned in effigy. Finally, in September, 1775, he and his wife left for England. (Some writers, including Boucher's great-grandson,

cite the date of departure as August; September, however, would seem to be the more probable date).

For the next twenty-nine years the Reverend Mr.
Boucher lived in England. He was for many years vicar
of Epson, he received a small pension from His Majesty's
Government, and he received a lump-sum compensation
for the property he had owned and lost in Maryland. He
also supplemented this income by tutoring and writing.
His *View of the Causes and Consequences of the American Revolution*, published in 1797, consisted largely of some
thirteen of the sermons he had preached while in America and while tempers were growing ever shorter. Polem-
ical as they are, they afford some insight into the mind
of the Loyalists. He also became interested in philology,
especially in obsolete and provincial terms. Three years
after his death his *Supplement to Dr. Johnson's Dictionary of
the English Language* was published.

This present work, long out of print and now made
available through the perceptiveness of the Kennikat
Press, was published by his great-grandson in 1925.
One of the more valuable personal memoirs of this period, it can be supplemented by the works mentioned
above and especially by "The Letters of Rev. Jonathan
Boucher" in volumes six through nine of the *Maryland
Historical Magazine*, and by Worthington C. Ford's edition
of *The Letters of Jonathan Boucher to Geo. Washington*, published in 1889.

These reminiscences seem to have been initiated by the
Reverend Boucher in the spring of 1796, less than a
decade before his death and more than two decades after
his departure from the New World. The editor of the
first edition indicates that the manuscript was in rather
bad condition by 1875 when his father (Boucher's grand-

son) made a copy, that a few of the pages were then missing and a few passages had been crossed out, and that the original manuscript had disappeared prior to 1925. The published version, therefore, was set from the copy made in 1875.

For almost half a century, historians have been aware of the importance of these memoirs for an understanding of the events that took place in Maryland and Virginia in the months before Independence. The descriptions of the Virginia he first knew, his characterizations of its inhabitants, his comparisons of Virginia and Maryland, are also valuable. The parts pertaining to his life after 1775 will prove much less interesting to American readers. Boucher was strongly prejudiced, extremely and probably unfairly critical, and a reader must remember that the manuscript was written more than two decades after the events being described took place.

In view of the scarcity of Loyalist memoirs and of Boucher's close contact with many people of importance, these memoirs will always be of value. Historians may well find them interesting as well as important. Boucher had facility for capsule descriptions such as this one: "Every Fitzhugh has bad eyes; every Thornton hears badly; Winslows and Lees talk well; Carters are proud and imperious."

Readers intrigued by personality development and by the influence of conditions and situations on prejudice and attitude, will be intrigued by such questions as: How did the poverty of Boucher's childhood effect his attitude toward paople of wealth and position? Might Boucher have become a Patriot if he had remained in Virginia and not come under the influence of Governor Eden and the Annapolis gentry? Why would a man of definitely lower-middle-class background find such strong appeal in the persons of wealth and education?

For whatever purpose one reads these memoirs, they will often prove interesting and sometimes valuable.

Cortland, New York   Ralph Adams Brown
11 August 1967

PREFACE

I HAVE been asked to write a short introduction to these memoirs of my great-grandfather, of which some extracts were printed in *Notes and Queries* about half a century ago, but which have otherwise remained in manuscript form in possession of his descendants. They give an insight into the character of a man who was considered one of the best preachers of his day, a schoolmaster of repute who was entrusted with the care of the sons of several noblemen, whom he accompanied more than once on the Grand Tour, then a usual part of higher education, and lastly, a keen politician, who had the courage of his opinions, whether right or wrong, and was able to express them with a vigour which for the time won him numerous enemies and forced him to return almost destitute to his native land. He thus represents the strength and weakness of English character in the eighteenth century, an age of firm friends and good haters, of a loyalty often pushed to fantastic extremes, combined with an inability to appreciate any point of view but one's own, of self-reliance and adventurousness united to much kindliness of heart.

The writer's early life in Cumberland is minutely described in the memoirs and need not be repeated here. He was born in 1738 of a Border family claiming Norman origin, but greatly reduced as a result of the civil troubles of the seventeenth century, and his early years were a continuous struggle with poverty, despite which he succeeded in acquiring a fair general education. The county was a backward one, and still in a disturbed state. When Boucher was seven years old, the invading Highland host of the young Pretender passed within a few miles of his birthplace, Blencogo, near Wigton, and the next year the little boy was taken in to witness the execution of several of the leading Jacobite rebels, whose heads long continued to grace the walls of Carlisle.

He had a very real affection for his native county, and after his return issued an anonymous tract with suggestions as to its better government and the relief of destitution; he contributed accounts of certain parishes and some local biographies to Hutchinson's 'Cumberland,' bought back part of the long alienated family estates, and married his third wife within the walls of Carlisle Cathedral, where he on one occasion preached the Assize sermon.

To return to his earlier life: In 1759 he went out to Virginia as tutor in a private family, returned to England in 1762, in order to be admitted to holy orders by the Bishop of London, there being then no English bishop in the American Colonies, and held cures in succession in Virginia, Carolina, and Maryland, besides carrying on a successful private school and working plantations of some extent. Mr. Custis, George Washington's stepson, was

among his pupils, and with Washington himself
Boucher began a friendship which extended over
many years. They frequently dined together, and
spent hours in discussion; and though Boucher's
loyalist views eventually led to a breach, when he
came to publish a number of discourses preached
during the years of the Revolution, after his return
to England,[1] he dedicated them to Washington 'as
a tender of renewed amity.' A number of letters
which passed between the two are still in existence.

The stormy years preceding his return to England in 1775 are sufficiently described in the memoirs, and this is not the place to pass judgment on
either party to the controversy. It may, however,
be recalled that political loyalty was felt to be much
more closely bound up with religion than at the
present day; and that churchmen took a much
larger share in political controversy without
offence.

On returning to England, Boucher was granted a
small pension by the Government in consideration
of his losses, was appointed curate of Paddington
on the western outskirts of London, and again
started a private school, which proved successful.
He had had no University training, though in 1774,
King's College, New York, had, unsolicited, con-
ferred on him the M.A. degree, but he had by diligent study acquired considerable classical and the-
ological knowledge, as well as a familiarity very

[1] *A View of the Causes and Consequences of the American Revolution.* 1797.

unusual in those days with archaic and provincial
English words. The later years of his life were
largely spent in an attempt to arrange these in the
form of a dictionary. A portion of this appeared
after his death, and some of the materials it is believed were handed over to the compilers of Web-
ster's English Dictionary. He amassed a vast
library which, at his death, took several days to
disperse. He was a member of the well-known cler-
ical club called Nobody's Club, and in 1785 was
presented to the living of Epsom in Surrey, where
he resided till his death in 1806. The patron of this
living was the Reverend John Parkhurst, editor of
Greek and Hebrew Lexicons; and in the 'Life' of
Mr. Parkhurst prefixed to the Hebrew-English
Lexicon it is stated that 'he made the appointment
because Mr. Boucher had distinguished himself in
America during the revolution by his loyalty and
by teaching the unsophisticated doctrines of the
Church of England to a set of rebellious schismatics at the hazard of his life.'

Another friend was his Cumberland neighbour
Sir Frederick Eden, a philanthropist who exerted
himself to improve the state of the poor, and also
published an amusing *jeu l'esprit* called 'A Vision,'
in macaronic verse, chiefly concerned with Boucher's etymological researches,

> '*O vicar, Epsomi qui nunc studiosus in umbra*
> *Monstrosam fillis cum queint etymology bookam,*'

but with some references to his past conflicts with
schismatics and rebels,

'Sermones nosti, Loyaliste! prechare toreos
Contra Virginios et halanshakeros Marylandos,
Auld Nicko sendens Whiggæos Americanos.'

A humbler friend was Mr. John James, son of Boucher's old chief in Cumberland, at first as undergraduate at Queen's College, Oxford, and later as Boucher's usher at Paddington. The letters which passed between Boucher and James during the latter's university course were thought to throw such a valuable light on Oxford in the eighteenth century that they were published some years ago by the Oxford Historical Society under the title of 'The Letters of Radcliffe and James.'

By his first wife, a member of the same family as the poet Joseph Addison, Boucher had no issue; by the last, Elizabeth Hodgson, who belonged to a well-known Cumberland family, he left several children, and among his grandchildren were Frederick and Arthur Locker, both well-known authors and journalists of the last century, and Edward Boucher James, fellow of Queen's College, Oxford, and antiquary of the Isle of Wight. It cannot be denied that his energy and perseverance raised the family to a position more nearly approaching that of earlier times.

The manuscript was in a mutilated state when my father made the extant copy, about 1875, and as far as I have been able to ascertain has now disappeared.

EDMUND S. BOUCHIER, M.A., F.R.H.S.

OXFORD, *May*, 1925.

O well for him whose will is strong!
He suffers, but he will not suffer long;
He suffers, but he cannot suffer wrong:
For him nor moves the loud world's random mock,
Nor all Calamity's hugest waves confound,
Who seems a promontory of rock,
That, compassed round with turbulent sound,
In middle ocean meets the surging shock,
Tempest-buffeted, citadel-crowned.

TENNYSON

REMINISCENCES OF
AN AMERICAN LOYALIST

THE AUTOBIOGRAPHY OF
JONATHAN BOUCHER

March the 1st 1786 (*Ash Wednesday*)

ITS having pleased God to allot to me an uncommonly various and eventful life, I have frequently been urged by the few friends, to whom alone I have thought proper to communicate anything of my history, to set down some of the most memorable circumstances of it. My dear wife in particular once extorted a promise from me that I would do something of this sort. This is the melancholy anniversary of her death; and therefore, besides being thus on a double account, a day of fasting and of weeping, it has to me now more emphatically been a day also of recollection and self-examination. In everything I feel it a duty, as well as my interest, to do whatever I can suppose she would have wished me to do: and therefore I resolve to begin these memorandums, to be continued hereafter as health, leisure, and spirits may enable me.

Whether I shall leave what I here propose to write behind me or not, must be the subject of future consideration. My immediate object is, the regulation of my own life. If hereafter there should be any to come after me, to whom I may see reason to think what I am now going to write may be of any use, I have to entreat them to read it with the same spirit with which it is written. I have not less vanity than men in general have; but if by the grace of God, which I fervently implore, I can but keep the resolution I have now formed of setting down with the strictest impartiality what may make against as well as for me, it will be very obvious how little my vanity can be gratified. With no birth, no education, no extraordinary talents, no rank or consequence in life, (and, what is worse than all, not only a checkered but a very faulty life,) what is there of which I can be proud? Nothing, but that I have enjoyed the friendship of men of great worth; and that I was the beloved and happy husband of a good woman. Vanity, I fear, has been my prevailing foible: in youth it is perhaps natural, and may have its uses; but in the more advanced periods of life it is quite out of character and ridiculous. I shall not have undertaken this task to no purpose, if, whilst I am employed in the performance of it, I shall more strongly impress on my mind how very insignificant all human attainments are; and that he only has done or does well in life who is duly prepared to die.

My family had been settled in a village called Blencogo, in the parish of Bromfield and county of Cumberland, time out of mind. My father used to mention a tradition he had received from his grandfather that they came from Normandy with the Conqueror, and had lands granted them in the North. I have seen old writings respecting the estate, in which the name was spelled Bourchier.

My great-grandfather appears to have spelled it Bouchier, my grandfather Boucher, and my father Bouch^r. and sometimes Bouch. This, he supposed, had happened from his having been deprived of his father when very young, and being carried into Ireland; on his return from which country, the people of the county confounded his name with that of another still more numerous in the county. My father used to relate many exploits of his ancestors in the Border wars, in which two of them had been active chieftains, and had for their services large demesnes in the Debateable Lands. In the Civil Wars the head of them (seduced probably by the Sir John Bourchier, whose name appears to the warrant for the execution of the King, and who called my ancestor his *dear cousin*) took the side of the Parliament, and lost, as he deserved to do, a large part of his estate by it. After this they seem never to have risen beyond that class of yeomenry, who in the North used to be emphatically called 'Statesmen,' that is, they were a sort of gentlemen-farmers, who cultivated and lived on their own estates. My grandfather's estate at the time he came to it, was reckoned to be worth about three score pounds a year. In that age and that country this was a handsome property, and entitled him to marry one of the three co-heiresses to Dryam in the Abbey Holm. Mr. Thomlinson, the lord of the manor of Blencogo, married another of them; and a Glaister of Abbey Holm, the third. Our estate by this match was almost doubled. I yet well remember my grandmother by my father's side who was sensible and well-bred. She used to speak of her husband as a man that would have distinguished himself had he lived. All that I remember her to have said of his person was that his hair was remarkably curled. He died before he was twenty-five, leaving a young widow and three children, viz. James, my father the oldest, Jonathan and Catharine. The widow soon married —— Lamplugh, who was a native of Dovenby, but who had lived much in Dublin, where he was settled as a cabinet-maker. To this city, with this husband and her brood of children she soon removed, and there lived and died without having any more children, or at least any that lived. It was not a happy match, and they did not thrive. Her former children were probably eye-sores. I infer this from her having never given them any farther education. My father was soon put out apprentice to a shoemaker; my uncle to his father-in-law; and their sister at a due age was married to Mr. Luke Stock, a hosier, on Essex Bridge, one of whose sons has since become bishop of Killala, and is a learned, worthy and respectable man. She died soon, leaving but one daughter, who lived to be a woman, but died unmarried; but I have since learned from the Bishop of Killala that she had brought seven children to his father. My uncle Jonathan, after whom I was named, set up in business for himself, married, but not wealthily, and had a family of whom I know nothing, though I have often en-

quired. He was known to and in favour with Dean
Swift, who made him a verger of Saint Patrick's.
This confirms what I have heard my father say of
him, that he was a man of some wit and humour:
but he did not thrive in the world, and I am afraid
died very poor, soon after my grandmother did,
which, as well as I can remember, was about 1749
or 1750. My father also married very young in
Ireland. His wife was a widow of good connections, and with a good fortune in Kilkenny, of the
name of Walker. He carried on a large and extensive trade in Dublin, and I have often heard him
speak of having kept thirty men in constant employment. But neither was he successful in business. I think this easily to be accounted for. He
was a lively facetious man, sung a good song, and
was fond of company, and of course was almost
always in company. Though he stopped payment
he never became a bankrupt; and soon after he
paid all his creditors twenty shillings in the pound.
This was not done however without dipping [into]
his estate at Blencogo, to which with this wife and
two daughters, he was now forced to retire. I have
nowhere ever seen so thoroughly obscure and un-
polished a village as Blencogo is. Had my father's
state of mind been ever so easy, and his income
also, it was hardly possible either he or his wife
should find themselves tolerably at ease in a situation so very different from that to which they had
been used. His wife hated the place even more
than he did, and grew fretful and quarrelsome.

Unhappy at home, he was much abroad, and indeed lived almost constantly in ale-houses, and
contracted habits of drinking. His estate meanwhile was gradually mouldering away; and his
wife, after losing her spirits, soon lost her health,
and not long after life itself. I have heard him say
she owned to him on her death-bed that she had
foreseen with pleasure, and had by plan and on
purpose, endeavoured to accelerate his approaching ruin. She had calculated that when he was
ruined and done for in England he must and would
of necessity return to Ireland. He always spoke of
her as a woman who possessed an uncommonly
warm heart, and a bold mind, rather than any
great vigour of understanding.

Her death does not appear to have wrought any
immediate happy effects on her then unthinking
husband. One of his two daughters was sent to her
relations in Ireland, where she was brought up in
that unsteady and desultory way which is too often
the lot of female orphans, and where she afterwards married. I remember her well, and as far as
I could then judge her character much resembled
that of her mother. Her name was Sally. She
married a man of the name of Young, who was a
saddler, and afterwards settled in Sligo, where she
died in early life. I have never been able to learn
what family she left, or, if she left any, what became of them. His other daughter, Kitty, was
taken care of and brought up by his relation Mrs.
Thomlinson, wife of the Reverend Mr. Thomlin-

son, Rector of Glenfield in Leicestershire. They, having a good estate at Blencogo, used to come down to it, generally once in a year, and Kitty with them. I have a pretty exact recollection of her, and think she was delicate and pretty; and I well remember how affectionate she was. She too, poor thing! married soon, and married ill. Mrs. Thomlinson was strict with her, to avoid which she ran away with Will. Wooldrege, their coachman. She did not live more than six or seven years after she was married; and dying, left three children, after whom, as well as her husband, I made all the enquiry I could, but to no purpose three years ago when I was in Leicester.

My mother's name was Barnes, born at Little Bampton, where her father was an honest and hard-working weaver. I remember her mother, who was a plain, decent old woman. The father died young, leaving three children, Thomas, who was poor, and died soon, leaving nineteen children; Barbara, who was married to John Waite, a weaver at Aikton, and who was a man of the strictest integrity, most perfect simplicity and purity of manners, and the sweetest temper I ever knew. He also left a large family, all in low circumstances. Anne, my mother, was a housekeeper in my uncle Thomlinson's family; where my father, then hardly worth a shilling, became acquainted with and married her.

This was not an equal and therefore not a very happy match. A better woman than my mother,

I believe, never lived, but she had, as was natural, low notions, which my father, naturally warm and high-minded, and now soured by his undone circumstances, too often thought lower than they really were. He should have recollected that they never could be too low for the situation to which through misconduct he was now reduced. I have heard them both declare that when they married, the estate that was left would hardly have sold for as much as would have paid the mortgages upon it.

I have often wondered how my father, who was a man of great capacity and abilities as well as spirit, could ever bring himself to sit down on so hopeless a prospect as that of retrieving his wretched affairs at so wretched a place as Blencogo. It must have been owing to his having by this time contracted low habits of thinking along with the low and vulgar habit of tippling and drunkenness. My mother had but one object in view, and one plan of attaining it. She was anxious to reclaim her husband, and to be able to maintain their rising family; and she hoped to effect this by unwearied industry and the most rigid frugality.

Full of these ideas they set up an ale-house, and my father also commenced village schoolmaster. And in this way they continued almost as long as they lived. As I knew them in this course of life, till I was nineteen years of age, I knew enough of it to warrant my declaring, as I here do, that I cannot think it possible their whole gains from both these resources ever amounted to ten pounds a year. Their little land that was left, and had been re-purchased (by a small legacy left to my father by a friend who died in Jamaica) could not, when the interest of the debt that was upon it had been paid, nett more than half that sum. Yet on this pittance they lived themselves, and brought up four children, two of whom they lived to see in Orders in the Church of England.

It is impossible for me now to tell how all this could be done. I remember only that we lived in such a state of penury and hardship as I have never since seen equalled, no, not even in parish almshouses.

It always has been, and still is, much the fashion of the people where I was born to bring up their children to be what they call scholars. My parents had this ambition also. At Bromfield where the parish church is, and which is about a mile from Blencogo, there is a little free-school, worth to the master about sixteen pounds a year. Here I was educated, if it be not too presumptuous in me to say I ever was educated at all. A Mr. Lowther was my first master, a man of abilities, and a man of worth; but he did not stay quite a year after I went to him. Mr. Thompson succeeded him, who was but an indifferent scholar and a worse school-master. Mr. Chambers came after him, who in every point of view was completely unfit for his station. My father had taught me to read almost before I could speak; and when at six I first went to Bromfield school and began Latin, I could read and spell almost as well as I now can. And had Mr. Lowther remained I have the vanity to think, notwithstanding a thousand disadvantages and discouragements, I should have been a good scholar. For I loved him almost as much as from my earliest years I loved learning; and he both himself had, and knew how to communicate to others, such knowledge as was not undeserving of the name of learning.

But as though it had not been enough to place me under bad masters (whose only recommendation was that they received no pay) I was not even permitted to attend them with any constancy. No sooner was I able to work than the necessities of my parents compelled them to make me work. There is no kind of labour at which I have not often worked as hard as any man in England, and, I may add, I have fared as hard. Besides carting coals, turf, and peat, I drove the plough, and wrought without intermission during the whole seasons of hay-time and harvest.

It is, however, an undoubted fact that both young and old I was naturally lazy and hated work. And though I then did work, and have ever since led a most busy and active life, I cannot deny that I never laboured but when I could not help it. This was so notorious at Blencogo when I was a boy, and was thought there so very bad a symptom, that I well remember how many prognostications were made that I should certainly come to an ill end.

Besides the avocations from school to which I was subject from my parents, I had many also from Mr. Thomlinson's family. Mrs. Thomlinson was a gentlewoman, being of the Winstanley family in Leicestershire; and tho' high-minded and apt to domineer, had a thousand great and good qualities, for which I at least should and do bless her memory. She, too, I fancy, was unsuitably married; and it was remarkable that they were sixteen years married before they had any children. They then had two sons, the younger of whom was christened by my father's name, James Boucher. Mrs. Thomlinson was pleased very soon to take great notice of me; and it was not to be wondered at that my parents flattered themselves I should at least be well taken care of, if not made their heir. All such hopes were put an end to by their having a child of their own when I was about eight years old. As soon as this child could well walk I was carried, and kept there almost constantly to play with him almost all the time that they were in the north, which was usually all the summer. They lived in a large old house called The Hall, at the farther end of our village; and every night at least I trudged thither through the dirt in my clogs or wooden shoes, which, when I got there, I pulled off in the stables, where I kept a pair of old shoes, with which I might venture into the parlour. When they went away Mrs. Thomlinson generally made me a present, which, however, I do not remember ever to have exceeded half a guinea. This bought me all the books I had, paid my cock-pennys at school, and also served me for pocket-money. She also used to give me her son's cast-off clothes, or, however, some of them; which after he was big enough to be breeched, could be cut up, and converted into a Sunday's suit for me. Two suits of his made me one.

This may seem to have been but a miserable introduction into life; yet have I long been in the habit of ascribing, in my own mind, to this chiefly all the little merit by which I can think I have at all been distinguished. I saw here a little of something that looked somewhat like genteel life, and which, while it inspired me with some taste and longing for it, rendered me not quite so awkward and uncouth as I must needs have been without it. It taught me moreover that spirit of shifting, of contrivance and management, and those habits of exertion, which I consider as fairly worth all the rest of education. Before I was twelve years old I had resolved I would not pass through life like the boors around me; and I had learned also in some measure even then to earn my own bread. I do not believe that in all my life I ever cost my parents ten pounds: after the period above-mentioned I am sure I did not cost them one.

In 1752 Mrs. Thomlinson died. This was a heavy blow to me. I loved and revered her, chiefly perhaps because she did not discourage my aspiring hopes, and would, if she had been able, have been happy to further them. I should have noted that the year before, Mr. Love, who was afterwards a celebrated comedian, was in the North, and for some months at Mr. Thomlinson's. It was said he had run away with Mrs. Love; and, being without money, he took to portrait-painting, by which he maintained himself and Mrs. Love till shortly after he went on the stage at Whitehaven. I was thought to have some talents for drawing, but when Mr. Love saw my attempts he declared, and with great truth, that my genius did not lie that way. The opinion he was pleased soon after to give on a translation of an Ode of Horace which I attempted, was very different, and flattered my patroness even more than me, because it confirmed her judgment. It was on this occasion I first believed I could be something, and therefore resolved I would. But excepting this little glimpse of encouragement from Mrs. Thomlinson and Mr. Love, I do not remember any other person's ever thinking or saying there was anything in me. And much as I am obliged to them for that praise, which, whether merited or not, determined me to try to merit it, I cannot with truth say I have ever since at all distinguished myself by any poetical productions.

It was not only less generous, but less judicious, in Mr. Love to try, as he afterwards did, to persuade me to accompany him on the stage. So totally to seek as I was in the world, so easily flattered by a little notice, and being withal not a little romantic, I am confident I should have gone with him even then when I was but fourteen, had not Mrs. Thomlinson, happily for me, still been living.

This was not the case in 1753, when I remember, owing to a train of very distressing difficulties, I was obliged to work, and work hard, the greater part of the summer. Even now I remember, that as I was reaping on a very hot day in the field called the Peaselands, fatigued and thirsty, I offered, with a fervour that approached almost to enthusiasm, a mental prayer, entreating God to direct me to some course of life more congenial to my temper and my talents. And I bless God after that year I never have undergone a whole day's hard labour. After harvest I prevailed on my father, instead of Bromfield, to let me go to Wigton School, which was about three miles and a half. I walked this every morning and every evening, carrying my morsel of dinner in a satchel. Mr. Blaine was in high reputation, and there were some boys of condition, and many of some learning. It was quite a new scene to me, and I might have profited much by the opportunities it afforded me, had not my father been persuaded to make me spend half the day under Mr. Stoddart the usher, to learn writing and arithmetic, by which he hoped, I should the sooner be qualified to act as a schoolmaster myself.

For three or four months I was teased with overtures of this sort; first at Crookdake, where I was to go from house to house for my victuals, and to have a salary of about eight pounds a year; next at

Raughton-head, where there was a sort of an established school, worth about twelve pounds a year. At length an offer was made which there was no parrying. This was a subscription for thirty-two boys at ten shillings each per annum. Accordingly on the 19th of August, 1754, I began in form to work for myself, when I was not quite sixteen years and a half old, having been born on the 1st March, 1737/1738; and from that time to this in one way or other have I led a busy, if not also an useful and a profitable, life.

I was the third of my parents' children: the eldest was John, who, like myself, was brought up to learning, but with somewhat more advantage. For, dissatisfied with Bromfield school, our parents made shift to send him, first, to the Reverend Mr. Wilson at Aikton, and afterwards to another Mr. Wilson at Allonby, both of whom were natives of Blencogo, and the latter a man of abilities. Here he did a little, and but a little, better than I did at Bromfield. My brother with an uncommon honesty of nature, and sure and steady parts, had no great quickness. He was always a sounder scholar than I was; but as it is impossible for any memory to store up every article of knowledge, I remember when any difficulty occurred, which was equally new to him and to me, I used always first to solve it. In point of propriety and regularity of conduct he was always my superior; and the people among whom we lived liked him much better than they did me. For he was orderly and quiet, whilst I was often in mischief, and still oftener suspected of mischief.

My brother also was planted as a schoolmaster: first, I think, at Aspatria; and afterwards at Saint Rouks in the Abbey Holme; and afterwards at West Ward. Here he trudged on, barely getting enough to supply him in the cheapest manner, even in that cheap country, with food and raiment, till he was of age to enter into Orders; when friends enough with great interest were found to procure for him the chapels of Wythop and Setmurthy, which, together, are worth nearly twenty pounds. From hence he removed to Wickham near Newcastle-upon-Tyne, to be curate to Dr. Williamson. Here he married a Miss Dawson, from Manchester; but hardly lived out the honeymoon. This was in 1765. I loved him most cordially; for with a most guileless heart, he had a very uncommon and childlike simplicity of manners. And his attachment to me was beyond example. We were indeed 'fratres fraterrimi,' and though I was for ever committing some fault or another I do not remember that we ever had even a moment's difference after we entered into our teens.

His widow was left with child, which, as well as herself, died within a year of the time that my brother did. It has often been suggested to me that I was legally entitled to what he left; but as this could not be much, and I was at a distance, and her friends never gave me any notice about it, I have never made any enquiries, nor done anything but write an epitaph for him, and send money for a plain stone. The epitaph for some reason or other which I have never heard was not put on; and the stone, I have lately heard, is now almost quite obliterated: but if I live it shall be renewed.

March 2nd

In his person my brother was neither so tall nor so stout as I am: but he was better made and more athletic. His hair was of a light brown, and his complexion fair and ruddy. His death was occasioned by a violent inflammatory fever, in the thirty-second year of his age. From our earliest years to the time of his death we kept up a constant and most affectionate correspondence.

For the first year that I was at Wigton I boarded at a Walter Stephenson's, who was a farmer and a maltster at Low-Houses, about a mile from Wigton. This was a virtuous and a happy family: they were good in themselves and good to me. The comfortable quiet I enjoyed there almost reconciled me to my lot; and I was diligent and faithful to the best of my power in discharging the duties of my station. I had also set up an evening school, in which I taught grown persons of both sexes writing and arithmetic. This added about a couple of guineas to my income, and better enabled me to spare about one fourth of all my evenings to my parents.

But this was too steady and sober a course of life for my active and restless mind long to relish.

At one of my father's merry nights on festive meetings at Christmas, when I was but thirteen years
old, a young woman from Wigton was there, who
though of no great note, so far excelled, in my eye
at least, all our country-wenches, that I fell de-
sperately in love with her. Her name was Kitty
Harrison; and her father had been master of the
Free School at Wigton. I made acrostics and wrote
verses on her in abundance; and though she was
older than I was, and knew that I was nothing, she
listened and was kind to me. But though my attachment to her was constant, even now that I was
become something like a man, she could not or
would not wait for me, and so married a dyer of the
name of Dalton. I next fell in love with a Biddy
Jefferson, the younger daughter of a Mr. Lancelot
Jefferson, who was a reputable grocer in Wigton.
This did not last long. She had too little tenderness, or perhaps too much prudence, for me; and in
no long time after our breaking off she married
Mr. John Wilkinson junr., a clock-maker.

And now coming somewhat more forward into
life, I had formed an acquaintance with the two
Mr. Matthewses of Wigton Hall, and with Mr.
Daniel Lightfoot, who were all lieutenants in the
Navy. Spending my evenings frequently with
them, I too frequently stayed out too late. My
landlord and landlady at Low-Houses did not like
this, and spoke of it to me, from motives of kindness I am sure, but in such a tone of authority as I
then thought myself too great a man to submit to.

On this I left them, and went and boarded myself for five pounds per annum with a widow woman in Wigton, Betty Hastings, who kept a little grocer's shop.

[Two leaves torn out here.]

It was, I fancy, only because nothing better occurred that towards the close of the year 1755, bent on leaving Wigton, I went to Workington in order to learn mathematics. I boarded at the Reverend Mr. Ritson's, who was to instruct me; and I was to pay for board and education at the rate of a guinea a month. Here I went through all the practical branches of navigation, and also land-surveying, in which I had much practice. It was an odd combination, and seemed ominous of my being afterwards to *compass land and sea* in quest of a little bread.

This Mr. Ritson was a character, and thought so even in a part of the world that is fruitful in characters. He was bred a shoemaker, and had, long after he was married, worked at his trade in a very low way in a low village. But he had a thinking head, and a strong turn to mathematical investigations. And having taught himself, he next attempted to teach others. This he did with such success and reputation, that at forty years of age Mr. Stanley of Workington gave him a title, and he went into Orders. Not long after, he was appointed schoolmaster at Workington, and minister of a chapel at Clifton, both of which together did not bring him in forty pounds a year: with his private pupils he made it about fifty pounds. And on this he not only brought up his family, but saved a thousand pounds or upwards. I remember indeed our diet was both ordinary and scanty. For a month or more that I was surveying land every day, and in very severe weather, we worked from sun to sun without eating or drinking; and I do not remember ever to have dined at his house when there was not salmon and potatoes mashed, or when there was anything else.

Conscious of my insufficiency as a schoolmaster, my main ambition and hope whilst I was here were to get into some employment where I might live by my pen. And I had made a little interest with a Captain Whitaker, who hoped he should be able, and promised he would try, to recommend me in this way in Ireland. But this project, and every other of the sort, were soon put a stop to by my receiving orders from my father to go and offer myself for the ushership of the school at Saint Bees, which he had heard was vacant. Saint Bees is about ten miles from Workington, and I set off on foot on a Sunday morning through the rain, and so got wet to the skin. I went with a thorough disinclination to the employment, but returned anxious to obtain it. This was entirely owing to the high opinion I conceived of the Reverend Mr. James, the master, an opinion which I never saw reason to alter. On my introducing myself to him, and telling him my errand, I fairly owned how unfit I was for his purpose. He examined me, and could not but declare he was shocked to see how miserably I had been educated. I knew nothing of grammar, nor of anything else, on any principles. Yet he was pleased to say he thought he could soon put me into a way of soon learning what I so much wanted. This was the second time in my life that anything had ever been said to me by any person worthy of regard that might lead me to think favourably of my talents.

With no character nor knowledge of me, and with all these symptoms in my disfavour, this good man engaged me; and I entered on my station under him after the Easter holidays in 1756. My salary from him was ten pounds a year; and entrances and cock-pennies amounted to as much more. The second year I got nearly thirty pounds. In all my life I never have spent my time, or lived more rationally, than I think I did for the two years that I was at Saint Bees. The school, owing to the mismanagement of Mr. James's predecessor, was at a low ebb: there were not thirty boys when I went there. Mr. James himself did not exceed me in an earnest and ardent desire to see it raised. We both took most faithful pains, rising constantly by six, and ending our labours only when we could no longer see. The consequence was I left the school with upwards of eighty boys, and Mr. James afterwards increased his number to one hundred and thirty and upwards. It is now again, I understand, sunk to about threescore: so fluctuating are schools!

In addition to my labours as an usher, I here studied hard. Mr. James was not only the best schoolmaster I have ever known, but one of the best men. Pitying my untutored ignorance, he humanely went through a course of grammar with me, corrected exercises for me, and put the proper books into my hands to read. One very useful regulation he adopted (and, I am persuaded, for my sake) was, on the repetition day, which was Friday, to change places with me; by which means I heard all the higher classes all that they had gone through in the four preceding days. To qualify me to do this in any tolerable manner he took the trouble, on the preceding evening, to hear me read the whole of it. By these means, and by his conversation, I learned more than I had done in all my life before, or than, I fear, I have ever since done, in the same space of time. What I ought to value still more is, that here also I learned habits of virtue, and such principles of thinking and acting, as could alone have supported and carried me through the many severe trials to which I have since been exposed. Mr. James married whilst I was at Saint Bees; and I had the happiness to live on the most intimate terms with both him and Mrs. James; and to lay the foundation of a friendship which lasted as long as life did.

To this friendship I am proud to acknowledge I owe much, if not all, of either the knowledge or the virtue which I have since possessed. In his own principles and practice he was upright and blameless; and yet was as candid and indulgent to the errors and misconduct of others as if from his own experience he had been conscious how frail human nature is. I kept up with him for more than twenty years a constant and an unreserved correspondence; and there was not a thought, word or deed which I wished to conceal from him. God forbid it should be possible for me to outlive my faculties, and so far to lose all sense of right and wrong as ever to forget with what patience he bore my teasing him with a thousand chimerical projects I was for ever forming; with what tenderness he checked my follies and my faults; and with what sound good sense, as well as sincere friendship, he endeavoured to preserve me in the paths of prudence and virtue! And would young men of warm imaginations and active passions, who are prone to error only because they are usually precipitate and apt to act from a first impulse, but behave so as to secure to themselves the friendship of cool, steady, and good men, they never could wander far astray; or, if they did, they would not so lose themselves as never to return to a better mind.

I had now become somewhat of a decent scholar, and, what was of more moment, a tolerably decent man, when early in 1759 Mr. James heard that Mr. Younger, a respectable merchant in Whitehaven, wanted a young man to go out as private tutor to a gentleman's sons in Virginia.

Tolerably sobered as my mind now was, the desire

to go abroad had still been cherished; and it seemed now to be confirmed by judgment, and was not opposed by Mr. James. He recommended me to Mr. Younger, and our agreement was soon made. I was to enter into pay on the day of my leaving England; to have my passage gratis; to have my board and sixty pounds sterling a year for teaching four boys, with liberty to take four more, on such terms as I could agree for, on my arrival.

I did not find it easy to reconcile my poor parents to this great enterprise. They knew little of the country to which I was going, and therefore had a thousand fears about it, all of which, however, were not imaginary. I was wild, they said: should I therefore by God's good providence escape shipwreck by sea, they seemed to foresee that I would make shipwreck of all that was good in me, when no longer in the way of being restrained. But the die was cast, my passage was taken, and nothing could then have prevented me but the impossibility of borrowing thirty pounds to fit me out properly with clothes etc. which sum was at last lent to me by a widow Messenger of Dundraw on my own bond.

My parting with my parents was most affectionate and affecting. We had prayers, and I rose up from my knees, mounted my horse, and set off without speaking or being spoken to. We felt what was too big for utterance.

I forget now on what day in April, 1759, it was that I set sail from Whitehaven in the Rose, Captain Rothery.[1] We had a tedious but not an unpleasant passage, though somewhat dangerous, as it was in a time of war. Availing myself of my education at Workington, I kept a reckoning, and drew a chart of our voyage, which my good-natured captain got framed, and I dare say kept as long as he lived.

On the 12th of July I landed safe at Urbanna, near the mouth of Rappahannock River; and soon after got up to the place of my destination, viz. Captain Dixon's at Port Royal on the same river, and met with a cordial reception.

[1] The following notes of this voyage in Mr. Boucher's hand have been preserved:

Some occurrences noted in my Passage fm Wt haven to Virginia.

Apl the 27th 1759 set sail in Company with the Curwen & Richmond.

May the 19th a most violent squall, lay to under bare Poles, & in ye Morning of the 20th fell in wth a large Fleet of upwards of 20 Sail.

the 26th were frightened by almost running upon a monstrous large Grampus.

June the 9th were chac'd by a Vessel from wc we wth Difficulty escap'd by Favr of the Night.

the 29th, being very near Nantucket, saw large Quantities of Grass and Reeds.

the 30th spoke the Sarah, Captn Montgomery from London for Virginia. He had been out 9 Weeks and 5 Days, & reckon'd as well as we in Longd 66°.

July the 5th were brot to by the K. George. Captn Benjan Hallowell, a King's Ship of 20 Guns from Boston. She reckons 70 Leagues from the Land, & informs us of two Privateers being upon the Coast, Ex Quibus, Domine, Libera nos.

the 7th at 10 this morning, after a violent squall made ye Land in Lat. 37° 48: had 12 Fathoms of water & fine grey Sands.

the 12th after being kept lashing abt ye Coast at last abt 7 in ye Evening turn'd ye Cape & got up ye Bay in Company wth a Bristol Snow wth Slaves fm Africa.

the 13th July by the Blessing of God arriv'd safe at Port Royal.

I was now in every sense of the word in a new world. The people, in their persons, manners, pursuits and modes of life were as new and strange to me as their country and climate were. There is however a happy pliancy, if not in human nature in general, yet in my particular frame of mind, which soon learns to accommodate itself to any circumstances and any situation. In a few months I seemed to be naturalised, and again to find myself at home.

Captain Dixon had long commanded a ship in the service of Mr. Howe; and had justly gotten a great name both for skill, care, and gallantry, having twice successfully defended himself against opponents of superior force. He married in Virginia; and by his marriage became possessed of a very considerable property in lands and slaves. On this he quitted the sea; and settling in Port Royal, he was then employed by Mr. Younger as his factor, and kept a large store, frequently sending home two or three cargoes of tobacco in a year. When I first knew him he was a widower, with two sons, of about eight and ten years of age; himself about fifty-six, but very stout and very healthy. He was a man of strong sense and strong passions; warm and hearty in his manner; sincere in his friendships and violent in his enmities; open and cheerful, and with sea-manners. Being hospitable as well as wealthy, his house was much resorted to, but chiefly by toddy-drinking company. Port Royal was inhabited in a great measure by factors

from Scotland and their dependents; and the cir-
cumjacent country by planters, in general in middling circumstances. There was not a literary man,
for aught I could find, nearer than in the country I
had just left; nor were literary attainments, beyond
merely reading or writing, at all in vogue or repute.
In such society it was little likely I should add
to my own little stock of learning; in fact there
were no longer any inducements; and all that I
read now, or during my whole residence in America was mere general reading or such particular
subjects as particular exigencies occasionally required. It seemed more necessary to furnish myself with that kind of knowledge which was most
in request in the country in which my lot seemed
to be cast. Accordingly I gave much attention
to all the various businesses of a plantation: I gave
still more attention to trade, and some to the practice of physic and law. It had been well had these
engrossed my attention, but, possessing as I do
great ductility and pliancy of temper, I too soon
and too much gave in to the prevailing idle cus-
toms of the country. I was engaged in many silly
frolics with people as silly as myself, was very often
at balls and on visits, and almost constantly in a
round of very unimproving company. In all the
two years I lived at Port Royal I did not form a
single friendship on which I can now look back
with much approbation, though I had a numerous
acquaintance and many intimacies. [Sixteen lines
crossed out here.]

Before I left Whitehaven Mr. Younger, actuated by an uncommon liberality of mind, had empowered me to take up whatever goods I might want for my own use at his store at prime cost. He had also suggested to me that it might not be amiss if, as it was by no means incompatible with my other engagements, I were to give some attention to the state of trade, and from time to time communicate my sentiments on the subject to him. And he added that if, after turning my thoughts that way, I should be disposed to engage in trade, if he saw no reason to alter the opinion he then entertained of me he would give me all the encouragement in his power. All this I constantly kept in view; and when I had been about a year and a half in the country the scheme was brought to such a degree of maturity that, with Captain Dixon's entire approbation, a cargo of goods for the purpose was actually ordered from Whitehaven, and a house taken in Falmouth for me to open a store in, in the autumn of 1761. Two very untoward accidents blasted all these fair prospects, which I had long been looking on as the most rational, best-founded and most promising of any I had ever formed. [Eight lines crossed out.]

This was a vexatious circumstance to him: he was nearly sixty years of age, and besides was just at that time negotiating a very advantageous match with a widow Washington, who lived on Machotac Creek, Potomac; and I had been serviceable to him in his courtship. [Four lines crossed out here.] Puzzled beyond measure, and almost distracted, the Captain at length spoke to me on the subject; and after much *humming and haing*, hoped to allure me to father the child at least, if I would not marry the woman, by holding out some tempting prospects of gain, chiefly in the way of trade. I resented his overtures, and rejected them with scorn; and so did Carpenter, to whom also he had the weakness to make similar offers.

Disappointed, vexed, and ashamed of himself, he was weak and wicked enough to try to throw all the blame on me, and we never afterwards were perfectly cordial friends. In a vindictive fit he even wrote to Mr. Younger that circumstances were changed and discouraging; and that therefore it would by no means answer for him then to enlarge his trade. It was some time before I knew of this last step; and when I did, I was restrained by a sort of sense of honour from informing Mr. Younger of the true motives of this change of opinion. This was the less necessary, as very soon after Mr. Younger failed, which effectually knocked on the head all my hopes of becoming a merchant.

I was now once more quite to seek, and as much at a loss as ever as to a profession for life. My thoughts had long been withdrawn from the Church; nor could my late course of life in any sense have qualified me for it. Yet happily as I trust for the future rectitude of my conduct, a train of unforeseen circumstances now led me back to

this my original bias, and at last made me an eccle-
siastic.

A Mr. Giberne was Rector of Hanover parish in
King George's County, and lived across the river,
directly opposite to Port Royal. I had of late been
often with him. He was a companionable man but
nothing more; and the only person with whom I remember ever in my life to have gambled. I had
once won of him upwards of a hundred pounds.
He was now engaged to marry a rich widow in
Richmond County, and the parish there being vacant, and offered to him, it was natural he should
accept it. All at once, and without the least solici-
tation on my part, or even thinking about it, that
which he was about to leave was offered to me. The
suddenness of the thing, and my deep sense of their
kindness, rather than my not knowing what else to
do with myself, determined me to accept of it. I
did so, and was to sail for England for Orders the
week after.

Relying, it may be, on my great prospects in
trade, I had not only written home to my parents
to discontinue their poor business, and that I would
make it up to them, but by living freely and in some
style I had also run in debt to Captain Dixon upwards of one hundred pounds sterling, notwithstanding that by the great success of my school I
was in the receipt of more than he gave me. This
was not quite the beginning of my being in debt.
When I left Wigton I was forced to borrow three
pounds to clear off old scores. [Line crossed out.]

On my leaving England I borrowed thirty pounds:
I now owed one hundred pounds, and wanted at
least one hundred pounds more: and on my last
leaving America I owed three or four thousand
pounds sterling. And this habit of running in
debt has stuck by me through life: I can hardly remember a time when I did not owe sums larger
than my credit might seem to be worth. All I have
to offer in vindication of it is, that though I was uneasy at the means, I always seemed to myself to
have some good end in view, which I thought was
not otherwise to be attained. Determined always
to raise myself in the world, I had not patience to
wait for the slow savings of a humble station; and I
fancied I could get into a higher, only by my being
taken notice of by people of condition; which was
not to be done without my making a certain appearance. How far this idea has succeeded is not
for me to say. I know it has often embarrassed and
distressed me beyond measure. It had been insup-
portable, had I not from the beginning made one
important resolution, and which I bless God I do
not remember ever in a single instance only, to have
departed from: this was, never to owe more than,
in case of my death, I should leave enough, in one
thing or another, to pay.

The difficulty that now pressed me was, how to
raise money sufficient to defray the expenses of a
voyage to and from England; set me up on my return in housekeeping; and maintain me till my
salary should become due. This was not all. My

sister Jinny, full as romantic as myself, having before I left England, gone to London to try her fortune there, not succeeding all at once, and without waiting for my concurrence, resolved to follow me to Virginia. I had just got notice of her intentions, and that she might be expected every day; and our two ships did actually meet in the river, when I barely saw her.

I was not on good terms with Captain Dixon; yet on my insuring my life for two hundred pounds, he gave me letters of credit for one hundred pounds more. I boarded my sister at a Mr. Buckner's, who were people of note, and agreed to wait till my return. Captain Stanley of the Christian promised to give me a passage home and back again gratis. Thus prepared, I embarked on board the Christian, about the middle of December, and about the middle of the following month in 1762 I arrived in Whitehaven after a rough and tempestuous passage.

All the little time I now stayed in England was one continued scene of bustle and hurry. I went from Whitehaven to London for Ordination; and Bp. Osbaldeston being then just come to that see, I was long detained, and much plagued, before I succeeded. A horse that I bought of Mr. Pierce of Saint Bees for six guineas carried me to and from London. I took out sundry books and household furniture, for which the shopkeepers easily gave me credit. And now I took my final leave of my parents, with a presentiment that amounted almost to a certainty that we never should see each other again in this world. I have at this moment my mother's image full before me, as she stood at the door, and, waving her hand, followed me with her looks as far as the eye could see: and I could now go to the very spot in West Newton lane, where my father last bade God bless me. Affectionate, kind-hearted souls! I trust your lot in yonder future world, whither I am pressing fast to follow you, has been, is, and will for ever be, as happy as your measure in this was hard.

.　　.　　.　　.　　.　　.　　.　　.　　.

One farther particular concerning this my much-loved father, should these papers survive me, it may be of some moment to record. Mortified and cut to the heart at knowing that the patrimony which had so long been in the hands of Bouchers had through his improvidence been wasted and alienated, he has a thousand and a thousand times charged both my brother and myself with an earnestness hardly inferior to that with which Hamilcar is said to have enjoined his son Hannibal never to be at peace with the Romans, never to suffer the estate to go out of the name of Boucher. I have always considered this injunction as sacred, and that a curse would overtake me if I violated it. Accordingly since the estate came to me, though I have again and again been in the utmost straits, I never once thought of selling it, nor have I ever received a shilling from it. So far from this, my father left it encumbered with a debt of one hundred pounds: he also left to each of my sisters one hundred pounds apiece, all of which I have paid, and have thereby pretty nearly, if not quite, paid the worth of the estate. I have also within these few years laid out nearly four hundred pounds in the purchase of other lands contiguous 'to it; so that the estate, though it never can be made fit for anything but a farmer, is now once more become something like an object.

It was a remarkable coincidence, though perfectly accidental, that I again landed on the 12th of July, and again at Urbanna. Captain Stanley, with whom I again sailed in the same ship, and with whom I had a tolerably expeditious and very pleasant passage, now thought it right to apprize me of a heavy storm that had been brewing in my absence, and was ready to fall on my devoted head.

While I was gone Captain Dixon and Mr. Giberne had struck up a mighty intimacy. It has already been related how much and why the former of these gentlemen was out of humour with me; and it should have been related that Mr. Giberne was much in the habit of flattering and being flattered. We seldom think unfavourably of another, without taking pains to impress everybody else with whom we converse with the same opinion. Out of favour as I was with himself, the Captain seemed to be uneasy that I was not also out of favour with his new friend; and so among much other trash he told the reverend gentleman that I had often and in public companies spoken disparagingly of his literary abilities. And some particular stories were told, which left no doubt of their being true. They were indeed but too true. It had been much safer for me to have called in question his orthodoxy, or perhaps even his moral honesty. He vowed a dreadful revenge against me, and to shew how much he was in earnest he began with telling Dixon of my having in a very ludicrous manner related to him all the affair about Dorcas. This also was in some respects too true; and as my folly and perhaps ingratitude were without excuse, I could hardly blame Captain Dixon for taking it in such dudgeon. He instantly wrote home to Mr. Younger and to Captain Stanley very high-coloured accounts of my duplicity, want of all honour and extreme worthlessness, cautioning them against shewing me the least friendship, and advising that I should never go back to Virginia. I surely am under infinite obligations to both these gentlemen as well on other accounts as for this instance of great delicacy and true kindness. They were confident the story had been aggravated or mispresented [*sic*], and so they wrote to Captain Dixon. Mr. Giberne meanwhile went to every house in my parish of any note to tell everybody of my unworthiness, and to put them on their guard against so dangerous a man, nay, he even made it the subject of his sermons.

As both these gentlemen whom I had unwittingly thus grievously offended were men of established characters in the country, it would have been impossible for me ever to have done away the dreadful impression which their representations of me must needs have made, had not a gentleman of the name of Thornton, with whom I was then hardly at all acquainted, merely from a sense of honour and a love of justice stepped forth in my behalf even before I returned. He had by great good luck been present at the conversation at Giberne's about Dorcas, and he declared that all I had said had been much aggravated, and that Mr. Giberne himself had said many things that bore much harder on Captain Dixon than anything that had dropped from me, many things in short that were not only ill-natured but unjust, from which I had defended Captain Dixon, but in doing this had unadvisedly told too much of the truth. This declaration of Mr. Thornton's my friends had made good use of, and the Captain was in a manner pacified before we met.

I was obliged to preach my first sermon before I could see either of my new enemies, and I prepared one from this text Psalm cix. v. 2 — 'They have spoken against me,' etc., in which, as private grievances were no proper subjects for public discourses, I begged leave to waive any particular mention of the cruel treatment I had lately met with, but thanking them for having suspended their opinions, and listened to me with candour, I assured them I wished to rise or fall in their good opinion only as I should or should not be able to disprove all the vile calumnies that had been so industirously propagated against me during my absence.

Soon after this I effected an interview with the two gentlemen. As to Captain Dixon I rested my whole defence on what Colonel Thornton had said, who I believed had told all the circumstances more accurately than I could have done. There appeared to have been some imprudence and an appearance of ingratitude in relating things which I knew he wished to have kept secret: these were, I hoped, in some measure atoned for by my having, as became me, taken his part, and by the circumstances which had drawn those relations from me, and for the blame which could not thus be excused, but which he never could have heard of without dishonour, I sincerely begged his pardon. This abundantly satisfied him.

In the other case I pleaded what the lawyers call justification. Confessing that I had been to blame in being forward to give my unreserved opinion where it had not been asked, I declared myself ready to abide by and defend that opinion. One allegation was that I had said Mr. Giberne did not understand the learned languages. I did not remember my having said this, but gentlemen of veracity had said that I had: and if I had not before I now did say so, and was ready to prove it. 'Here is a Greek Testament: choose any chapter in it you please, and if you render it into English I submit to all the shame and infamy of having grossly calumniated you.' This settled the point.

He affected to consider my proposal as childish and beneath him, and myself as a sort of a bravo or bully in small learning, because I had been a schoolmaster. To this I replied, 'This is a poor come off; your shame is complete: and as if all that has just happened did not sufficiently prove you to be a bad man, you now give sufficient proofs of it in not being confounded with shame. It is not perhaps of very essential moment that you are illiterate; yet you may depend upon it, though I should be silent, this story will stick by you as long as you live: but it is of very great moment that you could be so cowardly and base as thus to attack me when I was not present to defend myself. For this every generous mind will for ever despise you.'

This said Giberne was the most admired and popular preacher in Virginia; and had, not long before, preached a sermon before the House of Burgesses, which at their request was printed, and for which they returned him thanks.

I seemed now to have gained a complete victory, and all those ugly appearances which had whilom threatened such danger to me now turned in my favour. I even became popular; whatever I wanted I could easily get on credit; and people seemed to vie with one another, who should be most kind to me. In the autumn I took a good and pleasant house near Leeds, called Smith's Mount, furnished it, and commenced housekeeper, along with my sister Jinny. I also now resumed my former em-

ployment, and soon had half a dozen boys boarded
in my house.

11th March (the anniversary of my Nelly's funeral)

An incident now occurred, apparently of no
moment, but which, as it led to some circumstances
of great moment in my little history I must set
down. One Sunday, as I was riding to my church
at Leeds, on the road I fell in and joined company
with a stranger gentleman. He was from Maryland, of the name of Swift, distantly related to the
family of the celebrated Dean; and being a merchant his errand in my neighbourhood was to secure a large debt owing to him by a Mr. Orr, which
he thought, and not without reason, to be somewhat hazardous. I was happy enough to point out
to him a way of effecting his purposes, which
might not have occurred to himself, but which happily succeeded. On his return he spoke of my kind
offices and of myself with such warmth that next
spring four of his most respectable neighbours sent
four boys under my care. And thus began my acquaintance in Maryland. And it is very far from
being the only instance of my life in which *after
many days* I have unexpectedly met with some
grateful return for some common act of kindness
which I had forgotten.

I seemed now to be somewhat in a flourishing
way, and as I was very diligent and faithful in my
employment my character was soon established.
But behold, early in August I was seized with a

violent fever, from which it was thought little less
than miraculous that I ever recovered. It was late
in November before I was able to stir out of my
own doors. The year before, just before I embarked for England, I had had a slight attack, and
every year after of all that I stayed in America, I
had some illness or other, often severe and tedious.
I recollect with astonishment the long series of
sicknesses of one kind or another with which I have
been visited. No doubt it must have shaken my
constitution.

During this illness my countryman and acquaintance, the Reverend Mr. Dawson of Saint Mary's in
Carolina County had died. Port Royal, where I
had formerly lived, was in this parish; and my
friends so earnestly solicited me to succeed him
that, after some hesitation, I at length consented,
but not before the people of Hanover, who had
so generously chosen me for their minister under
many disadvantages, also gave me their entire approbation. They went so far as to continue my
salary a quarter of a year after I left them; an instance of generosity which I hope never to forget.

My chief inducement to this change was the in-
commodiousness of my present situation, and its
unaptness for a number of boys. There was no
glebe in the parish, but four thousand pounds of
tobacco were allowed me in lieu of one; which
would have paid the rent of almost any house in
the parish, had there been any other than Smith's
Mount to be let. This was a pleasant place, but

there was little water, and that bad, a circumstance always much attended to in that part of the world; and I had been of late dreadfully unhealthy at it. Above all, the house though a good one, did not suit my purposes; and as it belonged to a minor, then under my care, it could not well be made to suit me.

Saint Mary's was not a pleasant place, neither had it good water; but there was a good house, and another old one, which at a little expense, might be made such an one as I wanted.

To this place I removed, with all my now large family, early in the spring. And now, besides adding largely to the furniture of my house, I bought stocks of cattle and horses, and slaves, running in debt five or six hundred pounds sterling.

But my industry and exertions were extraordinary. I had the care of a large parish, and my church was eleven miles distance from me; neither had I yet any stock of sermons. My first overseer turned out good for nothing, and I soon parted with him; so that all the care of the plantation devolved on me; and though it was my first attempt in that way, I made a good crop. I had now also increased my number of boys to nearly thirty, most of them the sons of persons of the first condition in the colony. They all boarded with me, and I wholly superintended them myself, without any usher, for two years.

At this glebe of St. Mary's I lived, I believe, seven years; which is the longest period I have ever yet continued at any one house. I had a good neighbourhood, and many hospitable and friendly neighbours; and I had a great turn for plantation improvements, which I indulged to a great extent. Yet upon the whole I cannot look back on this period of my life with much satisfaction. It was busy and bustling, but it was not pleasant; inasmuch as it was very little such a course of life as a literary man should wish to lead. And though it was neither wholly unprofitable to myself, nor, I trust, wholly useless to others, yet I attained neither of these purposes to such a degree as I now think I might have done. It was the fashion there to drink freely; and as I was always of a social temper, and always had a numerous acquaintance, these too often led me to hard drinking, tho' never, I thank God, to intemperance. [Eight pages of the original manuscript torn out here.] as fell in my way relating to Theology. I was also naturally of an inquisitive turn of mind, eager to trace the causes and reasons of things, and, if possible, to come at the truth. Guided by this principle, I have through life made a matter of conscience when I had read the advocates for one side of a controverted question, to read also those on the other.

When I entered into Orders, in addition to Pearson on the Creed, Burnet on the Articles, and some general defences of the general doctrines of Christianity, I had also read some manuscript dissertations on sundry distinct points in Theology, acute, learned and well-written, with which Dr. James had furnished me. They were theses which he had collected, revised and transcribed, whilst he was at the University. Thus prepared, my subscription was strictly conscientious and honest, and excepting some casual waverings and misgivings of mind on certain abstruse and difficult subjects, I continued a believer and orthodox.

I know not how it is, but an ingenuous mind, I fancy, is always gratified by asserting, as it is called, its own freedom; which is done, nine times out of ten, by reprobating old opinions and adopting new ones. This looks so like a sacrifice to truth that I who have felt the force of such a persuasion am little surprised that many honest and well-meaning men have been gulled by it.

In the course of my reading it was little likely that such writers as Clarke and Whiston should escape me. I read them with avidity, because they were always referred to as standard authors, particularly the former of them, by the writers of the Monthly Review, to whose judgment I then paid great deference. By confusing and puzzling me, they shook my faith, of which as far as the doctrine of the Blessed Trinity was concerned, I had well nigh made shipwreck. Yet as I hardly well knew what it was that I wished to reject, and still less what faith I was to embrace, in lieu of what I might reject, I continued only a sort of a bewildered and speculative unbeliever, and my doubts in theory had yet no influence on my practice. Whilst I was in this frame of mind The Confessional was published. I eagerly read it, together with the Candid Disquisitions, and many other pieces, all in the same way, of less name and note; which made such an impression on me as well nigh to have determined me actually to renounce my profession. I did in fact for a whole year forbear to read the Athanasian Creed. What a pity it was that I had then and there no ecclesiastical superiors, either to point out a better way to me, or to restrain me in my wanderings from that good old way which I seemed to be about to forsake, tho' I knew not why.

I have the greatest reason to be thankful, that I really did love truth; which I am afraid some of my misleaders only professed to do. It was then not more my duty than it was my inclination diligently to read what had been written on the other side. And I did this with such care as for some time to have become rather a studious man. Besides Bishop Bull and Dr. Waterland I have read almost everything of any sort of consequence that has been written on the subject; but I particularly mention the two first, as writers to whom I think myself under particular obligations. Mr. Burgh's two excellent Enquiries were not then published.

In the process of this enquiry I found that I had lost myself by attempting to stick to the expressions and definitions of our Creeds and formularies; and that it was necessary first to obtain, if I could, the Scripture idea of the question from the Scriptures themselves. Giving up therefore all hopes of ever accounting philosophically for the modus of the Trinity (which is beyond the reach of human faculties) I now first critically examined the New Testament in the original language; and considered the sublimer doctrines of revealed religion, not as subjects of philosophical disquisition, but as truths or facts, which the Scriptures assert. In this manner did I *search the Scriptures*, with the single view of ascertaining whether they do or do not teach the doctrine of a co-essential Trinity in the one essence of the Deity; and whether they do or do not assert that Christ and the Holy Ghost are God, in the same sense of the word as when it is applied to the Father. The result of this laborious examination was a full conviction both of the truth and importance of the doctrine of the Trinity; *and I pray unto God to give me His Grace, that I may continue in the same unto my life's end!*

It was, I am ready to confess, no small instance of self-denial, thus to submit my understanding to the obedience of faith. My ruling passion was, if possible, to see to the bottom of things; and it was this, I suppose, which led me first to addict myself to those writers who attempted to reduce the doctrines of Revelation to the standard of my own reason. A man of any genius at all will naturally be fond and prone to frame hypotheses; and he is flattered when he thinks he has explained the manners of divine things, and the grounds on which they are thus represented to us in Scripture. And hence it is that many a man as well as myself has been misled by such inconclusive arguments as, in any other subject, he would soon have seen the fallacy of.

Nor is it in the mysterious doctrines of faith only that human pride is found so much stronger than human reason. Deductions equally licentious and wild have been drawn from boldly speculating on the phenomena of Nature as on the Articles of faith. Not that we are not both allowed and required to examine both with all possible care by the exertion of all our faculties. Still, however, in both cases caution and reverence will be found necessary, because there are infinite particulars in both that lie infinitely beyond the reach of our abilities. Thus, for instance, no human powers are able to conceive *how* the Unity, Man, can consist of soul, spirit, and body, any more than they can conceive *how* the Unity, God, can consist of Father, Son, and Holy Ghost. And that God and Man should be so united as to constitute one Person actuated by the Divinity, is, in my humble opinion, not a whit more intelligible than it is, that the spirit of a man should be so united to his body as to move the whole or any part of it by the mere act of volition. In both Nature and Revelation therefore we must chiefly, if not wholly, be contented with the knowledge of facts, together with what we can find out of their designs and connexions, without speculating much farther. For it seems to be one great end of all God's discoveries both in Nature and in Grace, to mortify our pride and self-sufficiency; to make us deeply sensible of our dependence on Him; and above all to engage us to *live by faith and not by sight*, and in the practice of piety and virtue, in which alone all our merit, and all our happiness, consists.

My delusions in this way did not, I think, last much more than a year. I returned to the regular exercise of my duty; and, I thank God, have ever since been an orthodox and diligent parish priest. And it is the greatest consolation to me to reflect that amid all the changes and chances of a very erroneous life I have never been greatly deficient in faithfully discharging my professional duties.

It might, for aught I know, somewhat contribute to the bringing me back to a better mind, that the country happened much about that time to be greatly overrun with a number of sectaries. They had in a manner taken possession of two neighbouring parishes, in one of which there was no minister, and in the other a weak minister of a bad life. In my own parish I remember with pride and comfort I had not a single dissenter of any denomination. Some of the thoughtful people of those less happy parishes applied to me to go amongst them, and endeavour to check the delusion. Accordingly I prepared some sermons which I delivered among them, and by the blessing of God with such effect, that many who had been decoyed from the Church returned to it; and so, finding their congregations fall off, their leaders soon left them. I attributed much of my success in this to my avoiding all disputation with their ministers, whom I spoke of as beneath such condescension, on the score of their ignorance and their impudence. And when one of them publicly challenged me to a public debate I declined it, but at the same time set up one Daniel Barksdale, a carpenter in my parish, who had a good front and a voluble tongue, and whom therefore I easily qualified to defeat his opponent, as he effectually did. And I am still persuaded that this method of treating the preachers with well-judged ridicule and contempt, and their followers with gentleness, persuasion and attention, is a good one.

I now found it necessary to have an assistant, as I had thirty boys. I accordingly engaged a Mr. Lewis, the son of a respectable gentleman in Augusta County; and after him a Mr. Maddison [Madison], who was pert and petulant, but who has since become the President of William and Mary College. On my sister's going to England I also then had a housekeeper, having now so very extensive an acquaintance, that in addition to my very large family there was hardly a day in which I had not company.

Among my boys I had the son-in-law of the since so celebrated General Washington; and this laid the foundation of a very particular intimacy and friendship, which lasted till we finally separated, never to unite again, on our taking different sides in the late troubles.

Mr. Washington was the second of five sons of parents distinguished neither for their rank nor fortune. Lawrence, their eldest son, became a soldier, and went on the expedition to Carthagena; where, getting into some scrape with a brother officer, it was said he did not acquit himself quite so well as he ought, and so sold out. Soon after which he died at Barbadoes. George who, like most people thereabouts at that time, had no other education than reading, writing and accounts, which he was taught by a convict servant whom his father bought for a schoolmaster, first set out in the world as Surveyor of Orange County, an appointment of about half the value of a Virginia Rectory, i.e. perhaps one hundred pounds a year. When the French made encroachments on our western frontier in 1754, this Washington was sent out to examine on the spot how far what was alleged was true, and to remonstrate on the occasion. He published his journal on this occasion, which, in Virginia at least, drew on him some ridicule. Yet when soon after a regiment was raised in Virginia, he had interest enough to be appointed the Lieutenant Colonel of it, or rather, I believe, at first the Major only. A Colonel Jefferson, who had formerly been grammar master in the College, commanded the regiment, and a Colonel Muse who had been a sergeant, and therefore knew something of military discipline and exercise, was the second in command. Jefferson soon died, and Muse was disgraced, from some imputations of cowardice; so that the command devolved on Mr. Washington. At Braddock's defeat, and every subsequent occasion throughout the war, he acquitted himself much in the same manner as in my judgment he has since done, i.e. decently, but never greatly. I did know Mr. Washington well; and tho' occasions may call forth traits of character that never would have been discovered in the more sequestered scenes of life, I cannot conceive how he could, otherwise than through the interested representations of party, have ever been spoken of as a great man. He is shy, silent, stern, slow and cautious, but has no quickness of parts, extraordinary penetration, nor an elevated style of thinking. In his moral character he is regular, temperate, strictly just and honest (excepting that as a Virginian, he has lately found out that there is no moral turpitude in not paying what he confesses he owes to a British creditor) and, as I always thought, religious: having heretofore been pretty constant, and even exemplary, in his attendance on public worship in the Church of England. But he seems to have nothing generous or affectionate in his nature. Just before the close of the last war he married the widow Custis, and thus came into the possession of her large jointure. He never had any children; and lived very much like a gentleman at Mount-Vernon in Fairfax County, where the most distinguished part of his character was that he was an admirable farmer.

About a year before my sister's returning to England I had also become acquainted with the Reverend Mr. Henry Addison of Prince George's County in Maryland; an event which led to others of the greatest moment in all the subsequent years of my life.

He had heard of me from my Maryland friends; and came over, accompanied by the Reverend Mr. Brooks, who knew me, to see and judge for himself how far it would be right to place his two sons under my care. I soon after had them both, and two others along with them.

Mr. Addison was descended from ancestors who were respectable, in Cumberland, and of the same family as the celebrated Secretary of his name. He himself was a third son; and had, as well as his two brothers, been educated under Mr. Wilkinson, an excellent scholar, whom Lord Lonsdale had engaged to teach his nephews at Lowther Hall. The eldest son, John, in due time succeeded to the paternal estate at Oxen-Hill, which is the most pleasantly situated and circumstanced, and in all respects the most desirable of any I have ever seen in any part of the world. Thomas, the second son, went into the Army; and after the siege of Quebec, in which he so distinguished himself that Lord Townsend made him a present of his own sword, and he also enjoyed the friendship of, and corresponded with, Colonel Barre. He sold out his Majority in the 29th Regiment, and retired to his little patrimony near Oxen-Hill. He was a gallant soldier, and much of a gentleman; yet finding himself, I suppose, moped and melancholy in his retirement, so very different from the course of life to which he had so long been accustomed, it is most melancholy to think how soon and totally he gave himself up to habits of sottishness and vulgarity. And what appeared to me still more extraordinary, he became addicted not only to low company, but to the worst kind of liquor; intoxicating himself daily with a vile spirituous distillation from molasses, there called New England Rum. It was impossible for any constitution to hold out against such constant intemperance; he died in about five years after he withdrew from the world, leaving to his two nieces, the daughters of his elder brother, as much land as they sold for two thousand pounds, and the rest of his handsome estate to their elder brother. John, the eldest son, was also an irregular and intemperate man, and of course died young, leaving behind him two sons and two daughters. Henry finished his education at Queen's College in Oxford; from whence returning in Orders to his native country, he was soon preferred to the Rectory of his native parish, one of the best in the province, being estimated, communibus annis, at five or six hundred a year. He married into the Dulany family, and had two sons and a daughter. In no part of the world have I ever met with a better scholar, or a more sensible man. Yet his lot having also fallen in a country where literature was not at all in vogue, he too, like myself, seemed to have renounced all literary pursuits; and reading little or nothing, was degenerating fast into a mere humdrum country parson. After our acquaintance, which soon became most intimate and cordial, we

did occasionally shame one another into a somewhat better practice. I began to collect books, and
soon had a large library: and tho' his education had
been as good, as mine had been bad, and of course
he was a better scholar than ever I could hope to
be, yet he had such a confirmed habit of indolence,
a habit not easily avoided in those warm latitudes,
that with all my employments and (what was
worse) with all my turn for company, I read and
studied infinitely more than he did. Mr. Addison
was rich, and I am sorry to add, was tenacious of
money.

On my becoming acquainted with him, two
points, both of them of great consequence to me,
soon engaged his attention. These were, the dis-
engaging me from my attachment to Mrs. Chase,
whose innocency he always suspected, and the pro-
curing me preferment in Maryland, where Church
preferment was so much better than it was in Virginia. It has already been related what his success
was in his first purpose; for it was almost wholly
owing to his judgment and industry that I was enabled to unravel so very mysterious a story. And
it may seem extraordinary that he obtained all his
informations through that very Mr. Smallwood,
who seemed to be much interested in their being
kept secret, and who little suspected that he himself led to their discovery.

The other great act of friendship which Mr. Addison meditated for me was not, as things turned
out, either so easily or so speedily to be accom-

plished as he had hoped. Colonel Sharpe was at that time governor of the province; a well-meaning but weak man, and much under the influence of a Mr. Ridout, his Secretary. The Dulanys were one of the first families in Maryland, and at that time in the greatest power, one of them being Secretary of the Province, and another, Commissary; both of them in the Council, both opulent and men of first-rate abilities. Mr. Addison, before related to, and intimately acquainted with, them, had married their sister; and thus it was easy for him to engage all their interest in my behalf. His own rank, family, and character indeed gave him a right to ask for a living, of all which the governor was the patron. He did make the application, which the Dulanys warmly seconded, and the result was that I was promised the Rectory of Saint Anne's in Annapolis as soon as ever it was vacant. This living, in the metropolis, is pleasant, tho' but of small value: but it was usual to give it first to a candidate who was from thence promoted to a better benefice, as they fell, and he had interest. Hence it got the name of Gradus ad Parnassum. It soon fell vacant; which when I heard of, to the great vexation of my friends and my astonishment I also heard that it was given away to a Mr. Edmiston. This Mr. Edmiston, it was alleged, had just arrived with such strong recommendations from Lord and Lady Essex, who were related to, and much connected with, Lord Baltimore, then the Proprietary, that the Governor, notwithstanding his engagements to me, could not think himself at liberty not immediately to regard. This did not quite satisfy my friends; but as there was almost a certainty that it would soon be vacant again they acquiesced. Another equally unforeseen and unexpected event a second time furnished a pretence for a second time disappointing me. The Reverend Mr. Bennet Allen of Wadham College, a man of some talents but no principles, was the friend of Mr. Morris, who, from having taken the part, and written in behalf, of the Earl of Baltimore when under a prosecution for a rape on Miss Woodcock, had become Lord Baltimore's friend. Mr. Allen had also employed his pen in the same reputable service; and hence they had both entitled themselves to some reward. Mr. Morris was taken care of here; and Mr. Allen sent out to Maryland with directions to the Governor to give him whatever he should ask that was in the Proprietary's power to give. There was no withstanding such power. He was soon inducted into the Rectory of St. Anne's; and in some time after was made the proprietary's agent; a civil office of high trust and worth to him, not so little as five hundred pounds sterling per annum. While he was Rector of Annapolis, the living of Herring Bay, an adjoining parish, became vacant; and this also he asked for. The Governor thought he could not refuse him; so that there was no way to prevent his monopolising preferments but by calling in question his right to hold pluralities. It was certain there had never been a precedent for such a thing: it was incompatible with any idea of duty, and would undoubtedly give much offence, and occasion a clamour in the country. All these considerations were strongly urged in some admirably well-written papers in the Gazette of the country by the Honourable Mr. Walter Dulany; and were smartly, but with little argument, replied to by Mr. Allen. He had been used to newspaper writing, and so, finding himself unequal to his opponent in the way of argument, he endeavoured to draw him off from his main point by sending attacks on other topics in the way of ridicule. To some of these papers I wrote answers both in verse and prose; and had the luck at length to get the laugh of the public against him, so that he was completely worsted. This mortified and chagrined him to such a degree that, meeting one day with Mr. Dulany in the street, he struck at him with a cane in which there was a tuck, which he also drew: yet notwithstanding this, and that Mr. Dulany was a heavy, gouty and clumsy man, he thrashed him soundly, merely, I believe, owing to his superior spirit.

In the heat of controversy some harsh truths respecting the Governor's tame and time-serving conduct had unavoidably been thrown out. These he resented; and to shew that he did, tho' he was restrained from giving Mr. Allen two livings, he gave that of Herring Bay, not to me, but to a Mr. Magowan, a Scotsman, and an entire stranger, who, it was shrewdly suspected, paid for it to Mr. Ridout. His apology to my friends was, that his promise to me went only to Saint Anne's, which had not been vacant.

This was one of the last acts of his Government, as he was soon after superseded by a Mr. (afterwards Sir Robert) Eden, who had married Lord Baltimore's eldest sister. The first ecclesiastical vacancy that happened under his administration was occasioned by the death of the Reverend Mr. Bacon, and was by far the most valuable in the Church. Of course Mr. Allen chose it: tho' as the new Governor by no means liked him, he contrived things so as not to give it to him till he had given up his lay office. And now, with no difficulty, I at last succeeded to Saint Anne's. This was in 1770.

My unsettled state in Virginia for the two or three preceding years, in which I was almost daily looking for a call to Maryland, had been of considerable detriment to my interests. I neither could form nor pursue many plans of advantage, as I might have done had I looked on myself as fixed there. At present this is matter of little regret to me; while it affords me much comfort to reflect that amidst all my cares and distractions I still attended to my pastoral charge with fidelity and zeal.

I now have in my custody a certificate, by which it appears that on the 24th of November, 1765, I baptized in Saint Mary's Church 115 negro adults: and on the 31st of March, 1766 (being Easter

Monday) I baptized 313 negro adults, and lectured extempore to upwards of one thousand. I question whether so extraordinary an accession to the Church of Christ, by one man and in one day, can be paralleled even in the journals of a Popish missionary. They were so numerous, because my predecessors, shrinking, I suppose, from the great fatigue and disagreeableness of the duty, had in general omitted it, on the pretence that the poor creatures were so extremely ignorant, and wholly uninstructed, and could get no proper sponsors. These did not appear to me to be sufficient objections. All knowledge, as well as everything else, is to be judged of by comparison. Negroes, when compared with any other class of people in a Christian country, are no doubt lamentably ignorant; yet I saw no reason to think they were more so than many of the first converts to Christianity must needs have been, and particularly those made and baptized by Saint Thomas in Africa; nor is great knowledge and much regular instruction absolutely necessary to baptism. The injunction to go and *teach* is ill-translated; it should be go and *disciple*, or make disciples of, all nations. And negroes are not indocile; nor is it hard, even in a few conversations and lectures, to give them all necessary instruction in the elements of our religion: and in my humble opinion it is injudicious to attempt to instruct them or Indians in its mysterious doctrines. I may add moreover, and with strict truth, that I had under my care many negroes as well-informed, as orderly and as regularly pious, as country people usually are, even in England. Corresponding with a Society called The Associates of Dr. Bray, I had set up two or three serious and sensible black men as schoolmasters to teach the children around them merely to read at their leisure hours, and chiefly on Sunday afternoons, something as Sunday schools now are here in England. I had in consequence almost every Sunday twenty or thirty who could use their prayer-books, and make the responses: and I had towards the last of my ministry there thirteen black communicants. I continued this attention to, and care of the blacks of my parish, who amounted to upwards of a thousand taxables, all the time I remained in Saint Mary's.

And I also continued to take boys, though, after my views as to Maryland, I endeavoured to decline it. Two of them insisted on accompanying me into Maryland, Mr. Custis, General Washington's son-in-law, and Mr. Carr, who afterwards married the sister of my wife. My parishioners, on my leaving them, gave me such testimonies of their regard as I still feel with the most lively gratitude. They not only elected a person of my sole recommending, viz. Mr. Abner Waugh, whom I had educated as my successor, but over-paid me half a year's salary, and wrote me a farewell letter full of the kindest wishes and expressions.

On my finally quitting them I made a sale of all my stocks of corn, tobacco, cattle, and horses, and such of my furniture as I did not choose to carry with me. To my slaves I gave the option either to go with me or to choose themselves masters in Virginia. All the unmarried ones chose the former; and the others I sold by their own desire chiefly to gentlemen who, having been my pupils, had lived with me. And now on taking an account and estimate of everything I had, I judged myself to be worth about seven hundred pounds sterling.

April 12*th*

I cannot at present recollect many other events of any considerable importance which happened whilst I lived in Virginia. I had formed a very close friendship, and kept up a constant literary correspondence, with the Reverend Mr. Maury, a native of Virginia, educated at William and Mary College, a singularly ingenious and worthy man; who, with his numerous family, lived in Albemarle County. By his encouragement and instigation I wrote some verses on the dispute between the Clergy and the Assembly, concerning what was called The Twopenny Law, which were well thought of by Mr. Camm, the chief advocate on the side of the clergy, a sensible man and good writer; and I revised and made remarks on some larger pieces, on that and other subjects, written by Mr. Maury and his friends; by which means I had the good fortune to establish to myself something like a literary character. Mr. Maury was of French parents; begotten, as he used to tell, in France, born at sea, reared in England, and educated in America. His particular and great merit was the command of a fine style. It would have been difficult for him not to write with propriety, force and elegance. And I have seen other instances in which this quality seemed to be in some measure constitutional. Americans, in general, I have thought eminently endowed with a knack of talking; they seem to be born orators. I remember a whole family (of the name of Winslow in Hanover County) who were all distinguished as speakers; and so were the Lees, and many others. And there is this farther peculiarity observable in those countries; that the first settlers having usually taken up large tracts of lands, these have since, from time to time, been divided among and allotted to their descendants in smaller portions; so that by this means, and by intermarrying, as is very much their custom, with one another, certain districts come to be settled by certain families; and different places are there known and spoken of, not as here, by any difference of dialect (for there is no dialect in all North America) but by their being inhabited by the Fitzhughs, the Randolphs, Washingtons, Carys, Grimeses, or Thorntons. This circumstance used to furnish me with a scope for many remarks, such as do not so often occur here. The family character both of body and mind, may be traced thro' many generations: as for instance, every Fitzhugh has bad eyes; every Thornton hears badly; Winslows and Lees talk well; Carters are proud and imperi-

ous; and Taliaferros mean and avaricious; and
Fowkeses cruel.

On his death-bed Mr. Maury wished to see me;
and I rode on one horse and in one day (a dreadfully hot one) upwards of a hundred miles for the
purpose. He lived but two days after I left him.
I sincerely regretted his death. And I regretted
it the more, as very soon after I also had the great
misfortune to lose by death another dear friend,
the Reverend Mr. Tickell, who was my countryman and a man of worth. I had long been afflicted
with ill health, and had had many severe diseases,
which together with my sedentary course of life and
unhealthy situation, were supposed greatly to have
impaired my constitution. And I was thought the
more in danger, from a resolution I had formed and
kept of never yielding to any valetudinary regimen,
whilst it was possible for me to go on at all. Mr.
Tickell was also unhealthy; and as, in these circumstances, we both of us thought it possible, if not
probable, that we might die soon, we agreed that
the survivor should take care of all that either of us
might happen to leave. I was now called upon to
this sad office of friendship; and accordingly administered; and after no small trouble made shift
to remit to his relations in Wigton, who were poor,
three hundred pounds. About forty pounds I advanced out of my own pocket, in confidence that I
should be able to collect it out of debts that were
due to him. But I never did. His relations were
more grateful than I wished them to be, for they

sent me in a large silver cup that cost fourteen guineas, with an inscription on it, declaring the occasion of the present.

The having this money of Mr. Tickell's in my hands drew me into another engagement, which was attended with difficulty and trouble. A near neighbour of mine, the widow of a Colonel Spotswoode, whose father had been Governor of Virginia, and a General under the Duke of Marlborough, had married a Mr. Campbell, a native of Jamaica, where he was supposed to have large possessions. (He was a sensible and an agreeable man; and we were good neighbours.) But they had been expensive; and of course were soon plunged into great difficulties. To extricate them out of these, Mr. Campbell said it was necessary to go to Jamaica. He did go, but never returned, having long since settled in Bruxelles, where last summer I called upon him, but could not see him, and where he seems to live utterly unmindful of his wife and Virginia. In two or three years after he went away his creditors grew impatient; and ere long, as there was but little of any other property to seize, all his wife's jointure was seized, to be sold during his life. Mrs. Campbell during her prosperity had been thought to carry her head high; and of course everybody, instead of endeavouring to alleviate her misfortunes, seemed to rejoice in her fall. I could not bear this; and so, at the sales of her effects which were chiefly slaves, I laid out not only Mr. Tickell's three hundred pounds, but two hundred pounds more of my own. And with the negroes I thus bought I wrought the plantations, so as not only decently to maintain her, but also in five years' time fully to repay myself: and from that time to this, though the negroes are still legally mine, she has had the sole use and benefit of them.

On my breaking with Mrs. Chase, my friend Deckar Thompson, thinking, I suppose, that I could no otherwise be placed quite out of danger, was very importunate with me to marry; and through his persuasion I did go and ask Colonel Henry Fitzhugh on Potomac leave to court his daughter, who had a grandmother near me, intending to leave her an immense fortune. Both the grandmother and Miss Fitzhugh, on my applying to them, referred me, as was proper, to the father. He soon cut me short, and knocked the whole project on the head, by telling me he should have no objection to me if he had none to the settlement which no doubt I proposed to make on his daughter. Soon after, this young lady, the first fortune in that part of the country, being in a ball-room at Fredericksburg, at which I also was, miffed, as was thought, by some other lady's being asked to dance before her, fell down in a fit in the public room. And on this occasion it came out that she had been all her life subject to fits. Dr. Mercer, a very worthy man (then a physician, but since a General in the American service, in which he lost his life in an action in the Jerseys), being in my confidence and my friend, apprised me of this circumstance, and congratulated me on my escape; so that I was well prepared what answer to give to overtures afterwards made to me both by the Colonel and his daughter.

It was a mournful and melancholy service to me to have soon after this excellent man and friend, Mr. Thompson, to visit on his deathbed, and to preach his funeral sermon, as I did in Falmouth Church.

19th April

On my removal to Annapolis the scene was once more almost quite new to me. It was then the genteelest town in North America, and many of its inhabitants were highly respectable, as to station, fortune, and education. I hardly know a town in England so desirable to live in as Annapolis then was. It was the seat of Government, and the residence of the Governor, and all the great officers of state, as well as of the most eminent lawyers, physicians, and families of opulence and note.

The first transaction of any great moment in which I was engaged, was the assistance I gave in a Convention of the clergy of the Province, in which, chiefly through my instigation, we petitioned for a Bishop. This gave great offence, and for some months neither the Governor, nor any of the Dulanys, even so much as spoke to me. Conscious of my having done no more than my duty, I could make no concessions; and when at last, thro' the voluntary interposition of Mr. Wormley of Virginia, we came to an explanation, I still insisted I had more reason to be offended than they had; for that, in matters of duty, whatever deference I owed to their opinions, or however much I was bound to them in gratitude for past favours, or by interest in the prospect of future ones, I could allow no man to dictate to me.

A very handsome theatre was built while I stayed there by subscription; and as the church was old and ordinary, and this theatre was built on land belonging to the church, I drew up a petition in verse in behalf of the old church, which was inserted in the Gazette, and did me credit. And this, I think, was one of the first things that made me to be taken notice of. I also wrote some verses on one of the actresses; and a prologue or two. And thus, as I was now once more among literary men, my attention was once more drawn to literary pursuits, and I became of some note as a writer. The Rector of Annapolis is officially chaplain to the Lower House; and the salary was but about ten pounds currency a Session, and even that ill-paid. It seemed an indignity to offer or to receive a salary beneath that of the doorkeeper or mace-bearer; and so I wrote a letter to the Assembly in as handsome terms as I could, that I would, if they so pleased, serve them for nothing, but that if I was paid at all I would be paid as a gentleman. This transaction also made much talk in the country, gaining me some friends and more enemies.

Three or four social and literary men proposed the institution of a weekly Club, under the title of

The Homony Club, of which I was the first president. It was in fact the best club in all respects I
have ever heard of; as the sole object of it was to
promote innocent mirth and ingenious humour.
We had a Secretary; and books in which all our
proceedings were recorded: and as every member
conceived himself bound to contribute some composition, either in verse or prose, and we had also
many mirthfully ingenious debates, our archives
soon swelled to two or three folios, replete with
much miscellaneous wit and fun. I had a great
share in its proceedings; and it soon grew into such
fame that the Governor and all the principal people of the country ambitiously solicited the honour
of being members or honorary visitants. It lasted
as long as I stayed in Annapolis, and was finally
broken up only when the troubles began and
put an end to everything that was pleasant and
proper.

Sir Robert Eden was a handsome, lively, and
sensible man, and I now soon laid the foundation
of such an intimacy and friendship with him as
lasted as long as life did. He had been in the Army,
and had contracted such habits of expense and dis-
sipation as were fatal to his fortunes, and at length
to life. Yet with all his follies and foibles, which
were indeed abundant, he had such a warmth and
affectionateness of heart, that it was impossible
not to love him. With no other man did I ever live
half so long in such habits of the most unreserved
friendship and confidence. We were constantly

together whenever we could; and when we could not we as constantly wrote to each other. And few men equalled him in letter-writing. With an income of three or four thousand pounds a year he was always in debt: and though he had great quickness of parts, and a large experience of the world, he was a bad politician, as being not sufficiently steady and firm. In this respect my connexion with him, instead of all those advantages both public and private which it seemed to hold out to me, became the source of infinite disadvantage to me.

The times were grown beyond measure troublesome: men's minds were restless and dissatisfied, for ever discontented and grumbling at the present state of things, and for ever projecting reformations. In Maryland the condition of the established Clergy was highly respectable; and being all under the patronage of Government they naturally were on the side of Government, and thus, in case of competition, threw great weight into that scale. The officers of Government were still better provided for; and by this support Government, which, however, neither had, nor could have, any object in view but the good of the people, had generally carried its points, or at least had preserved something like a balance of power. There, as well as here, the country and the people were divided into parties. Placemen and their dependants took the part of Government, but were always opposed by a faction, whose leaders were instigated merely with the view of turning others out that they themselves might come in. And in Maryland the popular leaders have almost always been lawyers.

This had long been the constant state of things; but it was now much worse. There was a fierceness in opposition that was unusual. They seemed to aim at a total renversement, and to stick at nothing to attain their end. The Church and churchmen either did stand much in their way; or the great placemen had cunningly contrived to place our Order in the front of the battle, that themselves might take shelter behind us. Some individuals of our order had been irregular, licentious, and profligate: this was made the pretence for passing an Act, subjecting us to a novel jurisdiction (as we had no constitutional control, by our having no Bishops) of a novel Court, composed equally of laymen and clerks. The provision for the Clergy was a tax, or tithe, of tobacco, the produce of the country, viz. forty pounds (or thirty pounds of inspected tobacco) per poll. This was thought too much, as in some instances it really was; and Acts were moved for to compel us to accept of a modus, or composition in money, greatly to our loss. For a long time this was withstood. And this disappointment so vexed its chief abettors, the lawyers, that in a sort of frenzy they now pretended the law by which the clergy claimed the forty per poll was null and void. And this opinion they published in the newspapers, offering at the same time to defend the people who, in consequence of it, should refuse the payment of their

taxes to the clergy gratis. The consequence of
such a step may easily be guessed; at first I received about half my salary, and ever after less and
less. A suit was commenced in behalf of the Clergy;
but when after infinite trouble and delay it was got
ready for trial, the troubles had then gotten to such
a height that we could get no lawyer to try it. The
pretence of its nullity was this. The law was passed
in 1701/2; and the writs summoning the Assembly
that passed it were issued in the name of King
William, who, it afterwards appeared, happened to
be dead at the time. Hence it was contended, that
there being an original defect, and the authority by
which the people met being null, all that they did
was null. And yet the law had been in force, and
observed as a law, for upwards of seventy years,
had been recognised by many subsequent laws, and
had been ratified by the succeeding sovereigns, as
well as by succeeding Assemblies. What seemed
most provoking was that vestrymen also were appointed by the same law; and two of its principal op-
posers, viz. Messrs Chase and Paca, were vestrymen, and continued to act as such. In all these
contests I was constantly and materially concerned. I drew up sundry memorials, remon-
strances and petitions, and wrote many papers to
the Public. And towards the close of it I was drawn
into a long, keen and wearisome newspaper contest
with the two chief demagogues, viz. Messrs Chase
and Paca, of which controversy, the most important one that ever I was engaged in, as the papers

written on both sides are still in being, all I choose to say is, that I was generally allowed to have the better of the argument, but they carried their point. None of the clergy who stood out received their salaries; the cause could not be brought to a trial; and finally after I left Annapolis the Governor, beset and worried by his Council to give us up for the sake of peace as it was called, in evil hour passed the law. I must do him the justice to own that when he found he could no longer resist the importunities with which he was urged, he sent an express to me, urging me to come to him; and that if I still stood out he also would. Unfortunately I was absent on a journey; and before my return the deed was done, and irrevocable. The sad sequel of these contentions will come in in its course.

Towards the close of the second year of my being Rector of Annapolis, where I had a good house, as we had a good company of comedians, it was customary for the people of any fashion in the country to come and see the plays. Among others there came the two nieces of my friend Mr. Addison, who, as they were also relations, stayed at the Honourable Mr. Walter Dulany's, where I often saw them, and where an acquaintance began with one of them which lasted till we were parted by death.

As this is the most memorable, and in my own eyes by far the most interesting period of my life, I must go back to mention my having seen these ladies twice before while I lived in Virginia. The first time was at a ball at Portobacco, where I was with Mrs. Chase. The next time was at their mother's house at Oxen-hill, when an event so extraordinary occurred, that, though it was many years after that I heard of it, I cannot excuse myself from the relation of it here.

The eldest of these young ladies, Eleanor, was handsome, sprightly, and a general toast. Everybody had courted her; but having excellent principles as well as an excellent understanding, as there was not one among all her admirers whom she could thoroughly like, she had rejected them all. About a year before she saw me at Oxen-hill, she had had a remarkable dream, in which she fancied she saw the man to whom she was afterwards to be married. And the dream made so strong an impression on her that she related it to her mother and sister, and described the person. What made this the more extraordinary was that at this time she was courted by a Dr. Rumney, whom she then thought of marrying, and whom she would have married had she not had reason afterwards to think very differently of him. When I went there with Mr. Addison, the servants through a mistake had told them that I was Mr. Brooks, a clergyman who was their relation. Miss Addison came out, expecting to see her uncle only and Mr. Brooks. But on seeing me she started, and was with difficulty kept from fainting. When, without her having been able to speak a word to us, she was carried back to her mother and sister, 'Good God,' she said, as soon as she could speak, 'Yonder is the man I dreamed of that I was to marry!'

Of this story, which is literally and strictly true, all the remark I have to make is, that its being extraordinary and unaccountable is no argument against its reality. Though I had seen her at Portobacco she had seen so little of me as not at all to remember me. On her coming into company again the blame of what had happened so oddly was laid on a bat that was said suddenly to have flown across her face. At that time her attachments were to another person, as mine also were. I knew nothing of her dream: it was years before I saw her again; and when I resolved to pay my addresses to her it was much opposed both by her uncle and her mother; and had she not possessed an uncommonly independent mind it is certain we never could have come together. Mr. Addison's true objection was that he wished her to marry a near and opulent relation of his wife's who had long courted her; and Mrs. Addison wished her (merely through a false tenderness and want of resolution to part with her) not to marry at all.

Queen Anne's Parish in Prince George's County now falling vacant, the Governor, unsolicited, offered it to me, as indeed it would have been a shame for him not to have done so. It was a good, healthy, and pleasant part of the country; and the parish had heretofore been particularly valuable because the tobacco (being of the yellow or kite-foot sort) was the best in the Province; but above all it was in the same county with my dear Nelly Addison, whom I was determined to court (though I had not yet said so either to her or anybody else) as soon as ever I should be in a situation and circumstances to render such an idea somewhat less presumptuous. Under all these motives I could not and I did not hesitate a moment to accept of the living.

On my going down to be inducted I had indeed a most unpleasant reception. The unpopular part I had lately taken respecting Government had set the people against me. They were in general violent patriots, and as I was considered as a sort of champion to the party they opposed they were taught to consider it as meritorious to oppose me. And besides this there was a clergyman in the parish, the Reverend Mr. Gault, a native of it, and of their own way of thinking, whom they wished to be preferred. Hence the very first Sunday I found the church doors shut against me; and not many Sundays after a turbulent fellow had paid eight dollars for so many loads of stones to drive me and my friends from the church by force. All these difficulties only made me take the more pains; and though I never made the least concession respecting either my principles or conduct I soon made a little party among them, and so went on with tolerable quiet though never with much comfort; for they were indeed a singularly violent, purse-proud, and factious people; so that in such times it was in vain, at least for such a man, to hope to be popular.

My family, besides my sister and myself and servants, now consisted of three young gentlemen, Mr. Carr, Mr. Custis, and Mr. Calvert, the eldest son of the Honourable Benedict Calvert, who afterwards left me to come to Eton, where he died. To accommodate them I took a very tolerable house (for in Maryland few parishes had any glebes) of a Captain Magruder in the centre of the parish, which my boys called Castle-Magruder. Into this house we removed and got settled just before Christmas; soon after which there fell a snow so deep, and which lay so long, that we were actually isolated, and cut off from all society but ourselves for full three weeks. It was no sooner gone than, full of the purpose of paying my respects to Miss Addison, I prepared to put it in execution. And my first step was to advise on the subject with my friend Mr. Addison, who, by alleging that his niece would not have me, endeavoured to discourage me, but endeavoured in vain. I then wrote to the lady herself, apprising her of my wishes and my pretensions. This letter, as I afterwards learned, she immediately shewed to her mother, who on seeing it instantly burst into tears, saying, 'I know, Nelly, you will have Mr. Boucher.' Her reply was, 'I think so myself; yet never him, nor anybody else, without your consent and approbation.'

Her conduct to me when I first waited on her was equally frank, honest, and generous. I told her with the most perfect unreserve, as well as I could, everything that made against as well as for me. And she was won, though not unwooed, yet with such a generous contempt of all the little idle tricks of teasing, too common on such occasions, as greatly endeared the conquest to me. Four or five months now passed in courtship and preparations, by far the happiest in my life. Her mother was soon thoroughly reconciled; and I have the great comfort to reflect that she often declared, and repeated it almost in her last moments, how resigned and happy she was to leave her daughters under my care.

And here before I come to that happy day which made me the happiest of men I wish to draw something like a character of a woman to whom I owe not only the chief happiness I have ever enjoyed in this world, but to whom also I owe almost all my hopes of happiness in the world to come.

Many years after we were married, on occasion of some little matrimonial debate, in which we had each spoken of the other with more warmth than justice, it was proposed by way of settling the point that we should each sit down and coolly describe each other's character. She would not commit to writing what she thought fit to say of me; but I remember it well, and will set it down with all the fidelity and exactness of which I am capable. As I was not many days ago (in a mood of tender melancholy) looking over some letters, papers, etc. which she had preserved as κειμήλια, I found the scrap of paper on which this rough sketch of what I had called 'Nelly's character' was written. It shall here be literally transcribed, and added to a very short account of her; after premising only that the conditions of our agreement were, that every virtue we thought proper to allow to each other should be contrasted with some fault.

At the time I married her she was just turned of thirty-three years of age, as I was of thirty-four. She was of a middling stature, and her person was genteel. She had been exquisitely handsome, but a long series of ill health had much impaired her beauty; yet her eyes still retained (and to the last retained) an uncommon degree of animation and lustre. Her hair was jet-black, and her complexion somewhat of the brunette. With a constitution naturally good, she had long been sickly; and this entirely owing to the ingenious mismanagement of a Dr. Brooks, (now dead,) a relation of her family; a man of worth and abilities, but too apt to specu-late, and in his practice to indulge in ingenious whims. I am convinced she owed not only the loss of health to this ill-judged tampering, but alas! the loss of life. Her fortune in money was two thousand pounds currency, which together with sundry slaves, etc., I used to estimate in all at twenty-five hundred pounds sterling. And at the time of our marriage, besides my Preferment, I was worth about one thousand pounds.

Here follows the character:

'The features of her mind, like those of her face, are not strongly marked, yet both are significan and attractive. Brought up under almost every possible disadvantage, and with no education, she is well bred, of a liberal turn of mind, and possessed of an uncommonly good understanding. I never in my life knew a person who had seen so little of the world that knew so much of it. She is as artless, blushing, bashful, and even shame-faced as a mere country wench; yet she dresses with as much taste, converses with as much ease, and acts with all the propriety and dignity of a woman of fashion. She was not formed, I believe, ever to shine as a great and distinguished character, even had she been assisted by proper culture; but she affords a striking proof that native good sense and solid virtue, as they cannot be wholly depressed by neglect and mismanagement, so are they the safest, and by far the most useful qualities a woman can possess. Her person is the exact emblem of her mind, neat, elegant and lovely, yet, like her relation's style in writing, all this ease and simplicity are the result of study, care, and a good taste. The resemblance indeed between her mind and body is strong, and seems to hold good in little as well as in great things, and in her demerits as well as merits. Beneath the stature of very fine women, her mind also with a capacity for any extension seems sometimes to have contracted itself to its circumstances. And thus, tho' she has powers to be a great woman she is contented to be a good one. She is a Christian and thoroughly devout, and this in so exemplary and perfectly proper a way that I find it impos-

sible to suggest anything by way of drawback.
Industrious and frugal, and easily contented, she
yet suffers much unnecessary uneasiness from apprehensions of poverty. Her cheerfulness, founded
in conscious rectitude, and supported by religious
hope, no sickness, sorrow, nor any other calamity,
I bless God, has yet been able to subdue, nor, I
trust, ever will. Yet she has a warm and irritable
mind, and had she not, it is possible she might not
have had all those dear virtues and merits for
which, even in these moments of fret and ill-
humour, I love and bless her. After all, and to
close all, the most shining part of her character is
that she is, in the largest sense of the word, a good
wife. And this is proved, not only by my thus declaring it, after being married to her seven years,
but by her having always attached me to her, notwithstanding that I am naturally fickle and unsteady, and notwithstanding that she is always
sick, so as that I spend more of my hours with her,
and always happily, excepting the said misery of
seeing her so battered by disease after disease; and
that I still love her, and ever shall, with the truest
and fondest conjugal affection; notwithstanding
that she has just been rating me so roundly, and is
now preparing to give me a character which she
owns she is ashamed to write.'

All this, though written in play and frolic, is
strictly true and just, excepting that I should now
expunge many, if not all, that wears the appearance of being exceptions, and add largely, as I

could with great truth, to the little, far too little, that is said of her great merits. What she said of me was given, not by way of a set or studied speech, but as answers which I extorted from her to my various questions.

'In person, inelegant and clumsy, yet not rough and disgusting; of a dark complexion, and with large but not forbidding features. Of a thoughtful yet cheerful aspect; with a penetrating eye, and a turn of countenance that invites confidence and begets affection. Manners — often awkward, yet always interesting; perfectly untaught and unformed, conformable to no rules, yet never unpolite; incapable of making a bow like a gentleman, yet far more incapable of thinking, speaking, or acting in a manner unbecoming a gentleman. Never knew a person of so low an origin and breeding with so high and improved a mind; a thorough gentleman as to internals and essentials, tho' often lamentably deficient in outward forms.' There was nothing quite ordinary or indifferent about me; my faults and my good qualities were all striking. All my friends (and no man ever had more friends) really loved me; and all my enemies as cordially hated me. Women, in particular, were apt to be pleased with me, because I had a natural gallantry and attachment to the sex which made them secure of my good-will and friendship; and this, more especially, if they were under difficulties and distress. No man knew the sex better; yet no man who was not quite a fool, had so often or would so often be made a fool of by them. Indeed, a man of sense is a much fitter tool in the hands of women than a simpleton. In most respects, when thwarted and opposed, I was obstinate and mulish; yet there was nothing which I might not be coaxed into. A woman might do anything with me. Even my most wrathful fits had ceased to be terrible to her, my sullennesses never were so, she could at any time laugh me out of them. In one thing she envied me; whenever we quarrelled she always observed the overtures to a reconciliation originated with me. Her more proud spirit, she said, could not, so easily as she wished, be brought to this: yet she had remarked that we never in our lives went to sleep without kissing and being friends. As to my conduct in life, it was of a piece with the rest of me: no man took more pains, or laboured harder, to earn money, but I took no adequate care of it when I had earned it. I always intended well, but often acted ill; and even my good principles and good sense seemed to be no sufficient security to her that I would not one day or other in some strange humour do some capitally foolish thing. She was at ease only in relying that I never would do a very bad one. What sort of a husband am I? 'The best in the world, and dearer and better to me than anything else this world has to give. And now, my dear *old man*, prythee end thy catechism; for with all thy romance and eccentricity, all thy foibles and all thy faults, thou art a good and a clever fellow, and I do love thee as much as ever woman loved man.' And she flung her arms round my neck, finishing the parley in a way of which none but lovers, and I may add, married lovers, can possibly judge.

Fond as I am to recall and dwell on every idea of tenderness in which she was concerned, I may be forgiven the setting down so many things in my own commendation, and forgiven the being pleased with them. They please chiefly because they were said by one dearer to me than life; who yet would not have said what she did not think. I have, I thank God, many less equivocal and much fuller testimonies of her affectionate regards. *Old man* and *old woman* were our *nommes d'amour.*

From similar motives I wish here to record a little *jeu d'esprit*, being the letter I wrote to Mr. Addison to announce to him my intentions respecting his niece, of which I happen to have kept a copy; and which I value, not for any wit or humour which I suppose it to possess, but merely because it relates to her.

DEAR SIR,

Ashamed and weary of this unproductive and unprofitable course of life, I resolve to commence planter. There is in your neighbourhood a charming little plantation, unoccupied by anybody, which I think would exactly suit my purpose. As to buying it, that is out of the question; it is not venal, nor to be disposed of to the highest bidder: nor, if it were, have I wealth enough to buy it. If it were to be sold for what it is worth, the wealth of the Indies could not purchase it. I should indeed like to have it seiz'd in tail, which as I am sure I should never be disposed to part with it, might answer my purposes as well as a fee-simple. However, I shall think myself quite happy to get it on a lease for lives.

Scorning the little dirty finesses of common chapmen, who have an idle way of depreciating the commodities they want to purchase, I will frankly own to you I think this tenement inestimable: and I know that I greatly under-rate it when I offer not only all my worldly goods, but consent to bind myself to its fair proprietor till death us do part, or longer, if you can make the Deeds of Conveyance to be longer binding.

O Sir! 'tis a delightful spot! in my eyes the promised land, which, in the best sense of the phrase, flows with milk and honey; and even in its present uncultivated state, in the fine poetical language of the Canticles, is a Garden beautiful as Tirzah. But need I tell you that we live not now in that fabled age when *per se dabat omnia tellus:* let poets say what they will, *nunc nulla est inaratæ gratia terræ;* or, as Cicero expresses it, *Ager, quamvis fertilis, sine cultura fructuosus esse non potest.* Now might I but be appointed to the culture of so genial a soil, novice as I know you think I am, doubt not but that *molli paulatim flavescet campus arista:* I should soon raise a little Paradise around me.

I know indeed these sweet fields are already

adorned or *enamelled* (if I may be permitted to borrow a fine word from that redoubtable literary
champion, Colonel Landon Carter of Virginia, who
has so many of them, that he may well spare me
one) with every flower of fairest hue; but flowers
must fade, and even summer suns will set. Ere
long the ruffian winter will arrive, whose effects on
the vegetable creation are like those of old age on
the animal, and therefore will soon deform all the
beauties of the year. Now I, methinks, happily
possess so much skill in botany, and have a turn so
to *cherish* these short-lived deciduous plants, as to
render them perennial. I think I can like the old
Corycian, teach them to bloom even in those evil
days when Time shall have shed his hoary honours
on the beds on which they grow; of if they die,
Phœnix-like they shall either revive or live, as it
were over again in young ones which I hope to see
springing from them. Yes, by my prevailing happy
art, I will so exercise the rising grounds, and so
fructify the irriguous valleys, that when neighbouring fields shall be parched by *solstitial* heats,
blighted by autumnal blasts, or desolated by Bru-
mal storms, I trust to see mine flourishing in im-
mortal youth, and equally bidding defiance to
summer's suns and winter's snows:

> *Sic iis nec vernum nascentia frigus adurat*
> *Poma, nec excutiant rapidi florentia venti.*
>
> (Ovid)

It will perhaps be told me that as your own country is now abundantly stocked with *planters*, who

are reputed good crop-masters, it would be incongruous and perchance unpatriotic to employ a foreigner. This is an objection and has weight. It would, I believe, have deterred me from offering myself at all, had I not recollected that many fine plants, so dear to you, were all raised from seeds and standard stocks brought hither from the very country from which I come. Let me not be thought to vaunt, when I observe that you have no reason to decline making a similar experiment. Animated by the view of what has been done, I eagerly anticipate what may be done; and now that, as K. Richard says, I have crept into favour with myself, I will pluck up courage and tell you, with the lioness in the fable, that you should regard not so much the quantity as the quality of your crops. I am not to be told how surprisingly things here shoot up in the shade; but what are they? weeds probably; or at best poor spindling plants, without pith or vigour. There is, Sir, a material difference between raising a little shrubbery of puny, short-lived, wayfaring sprouts, arbusta, humilesque myricæ, and a noble, hardy, and thriving nursery of true English heart of oak.

Yet why should I doubt to equal any of your country-born planters, as well in the number, as in the good quality of my crops? I have, it is true, like some other *fellows* you have known, too long gone upon the monastic system of husbandry; and I have also studied Plato's theory; but I here declare my resolution to renounce the former; and I do, ex animo, most solemnly abjure and protest against all the fine-spun notions of the latter as heterodox and damnable. Henceforward I devote myself, in obedience to the first command given by the Sovereign of the universe, to study only how to increase and multiply. Instead of the casual fruition of a stolen meal, which, so far from being sweet, as a silly proverb pretends it is, is, I am persuaded, always joyless and unendeared, my ambition now is, *dapibus mensas onerare inemtis.* O what a gratification will it be to me to see my table decorated with those loveliest ornaments, those olive branches, the growth of my own plantation, which Israel's king has promised shall reward the exertions of the man who is truly industrious in these labours of love.

Permit me, Sir, to suggest a farther observation to you on this point, which I believe to be as true in the vegetable as it certainly is in the animal world. As in the latter, so in the former, you should frequently change the breed, or, as it is commonly called, cross the strain. Accordingly you will never see a judicious farmer sow his field with seed that has come off a kindred or congenial soil. What a dreary wilderness must America still have remained had it not been for the importation of our European exotics, which some naturalists have remarked, when naturalised frequently thrive better than they would have done in their own native climes, better indeed than many of your own indigenous plants do here. We are told, I think, that with respect to this part of America, the only aboriginal fruit you have is a harsh, dirty-dingy-red or copper-coloured plum, which Miller calls the Guajacana, *sive sylvestris Indicus prunus, cum cortice nec* [1] *piloso, nec etiam in intersticibus lanuginoso, fructuque valde acerbo.* This is an exact description of our persimmon. In England, we learn from the researches of antiquarians, that till the invasion of the Romans they had no fruit but a still meaner plum, which Cæsar describes as being *vitro infectum, quod cæruleum efficit colorem.* This, you will remember, very well describes the sloe. Not many centuries ago, in the Northern parts of Europe there grew an immensely large forest of stately trees, known to the ancients by the generic name of Scythians. These for want of attending to the indispensably necessary expedients of transplanting, grafting, and inoculating, in time degenerated into a kind of scrubby oaks, not unlike your Black Jacks, then called Goths and Vandals. Some skilful botanists happily hit on the only means by which they could have been meliorated. They were transplanted into different soils, and engrafted on alien stocks; and from this heterogeneous intermixture the world has been covered with such trees and woods as are now its chiefest ornaments. *Et dubitant homines serere, atque impendere curam!*

It is farther remarkable of the plantations here, that being still but scions of the parent stock, they are in no condition to be torn from that prop and

[1] The Indians always pluck all the hairs out of their faces.

shelter which fosters them with parental tenderness, *ingentique ramorum protegit umbrâ.*

But to return, this little demesne (and in the petitionary phrase of Lot, is it not a little one? and there are many reasons why I should therefore like it the better, even though I had never heard of this excellent rule, *Laudato ingentia rura, exiguum colito*) having once been a part of your family estate, it is natural to suppose you may be consulted in the letting of it; and therefore as I set up for a candidate, I take this earliest opportunity of soliciting your vote and interest. Rating myself somewhat above your common riff-raff overseers or tenants, I disdain the stale artifice of obtruding myself on you by any sham certificates or lying testimonials. I was brought up under an old experienced English farmer, my ever-honoured father:

> *ad hoc nunc*
> *Laus illi debetur, et a me gratia major.*
> *Nil me pœniteat sanum patris hujus.*

It is true he never was possessed of more than two plantations, the former of which, moreover, he fortuned (as the lawn-sleeved bully of Gloster, in some of his things, is somewhere pleased to express himself) to pitch upon among the bogs of Ireland, a country of which let me observe *en passant*, that there is not in the world a kindlier climate for prolific vegetation, yet was he eminently noted for his abilities in this first of callings, as Varro entitles it. *Adsunt testes.* Imitating the solemnity of Hamilcar's vindictive charge to the infant enemy of Rome; and like him choosing to teach as well by example as by precept, *insuevit pater optimus hoc me*, Plough often and deep. This, you cannot but recollect, is in the very spirit of Tull's famous system, who doubtless copied it from the elegant farmer of Mantua, whose perpetual maxim is, *frequens exerce tellurem*.

When I spoke of ploughing often I would not be understood to have said that my instructor was so romantic as to wish me to equal the ploughman mentioned by Isaiah, who plougheth all day to sow. No, to everything there is a season; a time to labour and a time to rest. Nor by ploughing deep, did I mean to say that my father thought, or had taught me to think, there was any absolute necessity for going to the bottom of things. That perhaps is impossible: neither am I sure, were it not so, that it would be good husbandry. For I am not like you to labour to eradicate but to plant.

Far from expecting that my cares are to terminate when my plants are to be removed from the seed-bed, it will be the pride and pleasure of my life to attend to every stage of their future growth; carefully succouring them as occasion shall require, and diligently extirpating every noxious weed that may chance to shoot up near them. Nor will I cease my attention till they shall be advanced to such a degree of maturity as that I shall not fear their passing inspection.

I am well aware that there are too many in the

world who have a knack at puffing their own merits
beyond all reasonable bounds; and that though you
yourself may know better, some others to whom
you must attend will continue to consider every out-
landish man as an *avanturier*. And that therefore,
though you may forbear to ask, *Quid dignum tanto
feret hic promissor hiatu*, yet you may be urged to
call on me, as another great land-holder once did,
for a settlement. I could tell you of large possessions I hold in so charming a country, that it might
well pass for fairy-land, called Utopia; but as I cannot pretend they are famous for your country produce I waive all farther mention of them. Instead
of long lists of slaves I have a large catalogue of the
mighty dead, to whom I owe, and hope always to
owe (what negroes do not always procure) a good
living. You must remember, and, remembering,
acknowledge the truth of our old Cumberland
copy, that these are better than house and land, for
'when houses are gone and lands are spent, then
such estates are excellent.'

But *crede experto;* I wish for no better terms than
to be admitted on trial. And if, after a fair exhibi-
tion of my powers I shall be judged unequal to the
service, be it at the discretion of my fair employer
claudere rivos, and to dismiss me. O were I but
once fairly entered on the premises, and regularly
set to work *cum omni instrumento ad rem rusticam
pertinente*, that is to say, the *gravis ligo, vomer pon-
derosus, actoresque bini*, I think, I think I should not
soon be turned off. No (*absit attamen superbia*

dicto), the means I should employ to bring my enclosures into a proper tilth would, I am willing to flatter myself, be so satisfactory and grateful that, enamoured of my system, my lovely and beloved landlady would, in the emphatical language of Saint Paul, exclaim, This is God's husbandry, and declare of her tenant what he has often said of the tenement, *tecum vivere amem, tecum obeam lubens.* Imagination itself could go but one step farther in forming an idea of the supremest human felicity, and that is that she should wish, as I trust she soon would,

> *Omnes ut mecum meritis pro talibus annos*
> *Exigat, et pulchrâ me faciat prole parentem.*
> (VIRGIL)

March 28th 1787

We were married on the 2nd June, 1772. The ceremony was performed in the evening, and at her mother's house (as is customary in that country) in virtue of a licence given me by the Ordinary, Sir Robert Eden, by her relation and my friend, the Reverend Mr. Addison. The day was excessively hot, distinguished as such even in that country, where it is so common to have hot days; and in the evening there was what is called a gust. So that though it was a happy day to me heaven did not seem to shed its kindliest influence on the hour.

In a little time she went with me to my house at Castle Magruder, about twenty miles from her mother's. And here we sat down to the business of life with a resolution to do our duty and to be happy. I felt myself so in an uncommon degree, when in about a quarter of a year after we were married my dear wife was found to be with child. This happiness did not last long, for being busy in putting up curtains to a bed, hurt by the awkwardness of a negro she stretched herself to assist, and, as was supposed, overstrained herself, for that night she miscarried. And she was so far from ever being with child again that she never afterwards enjoyed any tolerable health uninterrupted for any length of time. We lived together pretty nearly twelve years, nine of which she used to count she had passed in constant sickness. What a life of severe trial!

Other troubles also soon came on us. The times grew dreadfully uneasy, and I was neither an unconcerned nor an idle spectator of the mischiefs that were gathering. I was in fact the most efficient person in the administration of Government, though I neither had a post nor any prospect of ever having one. The management of the Assembly was left very much to me; and hardly a Bill was brought in which I did not either draw or at least revise, and either got it passed or rejected. It is not necessary here to set down how such things are done: they were done in that Provincial Assembly; and I have not a doubt but that they are done in the same manner and by the same means in the British Parliament. All the Governor's speeches, messages, etc., and also some pretty

important and lengthy papers from the Council
were of my drawing up. All these things were, if
not certainly known, yet strongly suspected; and
of course, though I really had no views nor wishes
but such as I believed to be for the true interest of
the country, all the forward and noisy patriots,
both in the Assembly and out of it, agreed to consider me as an obnoxious person. And these, besides my public controversy, engaged me in so
many little private and public debates with individuals among my acquaintances, and with Committees of patriots, that for two or three years I
was kept as it were in a state of constant fever.
Hardly a day passed over my head in which my
mind was not put upon the stretch by some great
event or other.

Settled not pleasantly among a people who were
much under the influence of those popular lawyers whom I was obliged to oppose, my wife did
not find it hard to persuade me to buy a plantation
of her younger brother's called The Lodge, on the
banks of the Potomac. He was an improvident,
expensive man, and over head and ears in debt; and
being obliged to part with this his patrimony, it
grieved his sister to think it should go out of the
family. I gave two thousand pounds sterling for
it, though I had not more than five hundred pounds
that I could command to pay for it. The rest was
borrowed. To this Lodge I removed my family in
the autumn of 1774; having for a year before been
busy improving both the plantation and the house,

which I did at no little expense. I reclaimed at least forty acres of meadow land, and laid it down in fine timothy; I made new fences all round the plantation, and grubbed and cleared several large swamps; I cut a large mill-race of nearly a mile in length, and had contracted for the building of a grist-mill; I actually built a large tobacco house or barn; greatly altered and improved my dwelling-house, and fitted up a handsome library; and I also made, almost *de novo*, a large and good falling garden. The better to carry on and effect all these great works, I had, besides three good black trades-men of my own, brought a good joiner, a black-smith, and a gardener; besides five or six white servants, husbandmen and labourers; my family at this time exceeding seventy in number.

These employments were more congenial to my taste, and afforded me more pleasure, more rational pleasure I mean, than any others in which I had ever engaged. And I think I should have been well contented to have passed through life so employed, could I have been permitted in such an indulgence unmolested. But all this time the public troubles were going on, and increasing rapidly; and I unhappily was made to feel the calamity in all its force.

Besides these vast undertakings immediately on my own home plantation, I had now also embarked in various land adventures and others for the augmentation of my fortune: and besides the Lodge was now possessed of upwards of four

thousand acres of back lands, which cost me something; and could I have kept them till now would
undoubtedly have been worth as many guineas.

About this time also the eldest brother of my
wife died, leaving a large young family and a very
fine estate. He had made me one of his executors;
and this also drew down on me much business;
some of it very disagreeable, and which in the end,
was attended with very bad consequences to me.
He had let some large lots of land to some respectable persons, the relations of a Mr. Hanson, an
opulent man of that neighbourhood of great influence. These men committed, and had long committed with impunity sundry trespasses, which at
length I thought it my duty to put a stop to. This
I affected, and in the way of arbitration, when
heavy damages were awarded against them. This,
one might have hoped, sufficiently vindicated me;
yet as it was pretty certain that if I had not inter-
fered nobody else would, I have reason to believe
they never entirely forgave me. I inferred this
from their afterwards pursuing and harassing me
with such unremitting rancour, as a public man, in
the progress of the troubles, which soon enabled
them to obtain ample revenge. This was far from
being the only instance in which private grudges
gave rise to public measures. Such motives (in my
mind by far the most prevalent in all public commotions) lie beyond the reach of ordinary historians;
a circumstance that, among others, renders every
history I have yet seen, or expect soon to see, of the

late war, exceedingly unsatisfactory. I am not conscious that I should assert more than I can prove were I to declare that the revolt itself originated in private resentment. I have heard Governor Franklin, the son of the arch-traitor of that name, repeatedly declare he knew his father was stimulated to do what he did (and who did more?) by the indignities which he fancied were put upon him when he was examined before the Council by the lawyer Medderburne, now Lord Loughborough. And I could also prove, if it were necessary, that Mr. Hanson and his friends omitted no opportunity which their weight in the world gave them to frame and bring forward charges against me: whilst I am as confident I never gave them any other offence than that of not permitting them with impunity to wrong my orphan nephews.

2nd April

It affords me more comfort and satisfaction than I can well express to recollect that I have nothing very bad to charge myself with on the score of rigour or severity to my slaves. No compliment was ever paid me which went so near my heart as when a gentleman was one day coming to my house, and having overtaken a slave, asked him, as is common, to whom he belonged. The negro replied, 'To Parson Boucher, thank God!' And few things affected me more than their condition on my leaving them. Much might be said on this subject. Nothing is easier than to excite compassion by declamations against slavery. Yet I have seldom heard or read things of this sort which carried much conviction to my mind. The condition of the lower classes of mankind everywhere, when compared with that of those above them, may seem hard; yet on a fair investigation, it will probably be found that people in general in a low sphere are not less happy than those in a higher sphere. I am equally well persuaded in my own mind that the negroes in general in Virginia and Maryland in my time were not upon the whole worse off nor less happy than the labouring poor in Great Britain. Many things respecting them no doubt were wrong; but this is saying no more than might be said of the poor of these kingdoms. I used to think it remarkable, but when well considered it is not perhaps at all so, that the most clamorous advocates for liberty were uniformly the harshest and worst masters of slaves. This might be farther illustrated and proved by a reference to the different nations who possess slaves, as those under a despotic government are known to be much better treated than those under republics. Thus the Spaniards are the best masters of slaves, and the Dutch the worst. As for the abstract question of the right that one part of mankind have to make slaves of another, that would carry me a length very unsuitable to these private memoirs: suffice it to say that I think the discussion of it of less moment to the interests of mankind in general than is commonly imagined. Slavery is not one of the most intolerable evils incident to humanity, even to slaves; I have known thousands of slaves as well-informed, as well-clad, as well-fed, and in every respect as well off as nine out of ten of the poor in every kingdom of Europe are. Nor is the possession of slaves so desirable an acquisition as may be imagined: if a wrong be done them, as I question not there is, in making them slaves, their owners are probably sufficiently punished by the unpleasant nature of their services. I remember a gentleman of Virginia, the owner of many slaves, used to say that the passage of Scripture in which the difficulty of a rich man's entering into the Kingdom of Heaven is spoken of must certainly have alluded to those who were rich in slaves. As to the effect which such a motley mixtrue of different people and different conditions who never can thoroughly coalesce must needs have on political society, the investigation of it must also here be declined. It is however a matter of no ordinary moment to those who are now so fond of speculating on the future condition of America; as well as the justice and policy due to another very remarkable race of people there, I mean the Indians. This extraordinary variety, which is without a parallel in any other government, either ancient or modern, always struck me as a thing that had a great influence on the manners and turn of thinking of the people of that country. Though all nations no doubt are of one blood and kindred, and though therefore in the eye of reason and revelation every man is allied to every man as his neighbour and his

brother, yet every observant man who has resided
in America must have seen that men are less attached to each other, and the bond of social or
political union is looser there than in almost any
other country. Man is a creature of habits; when
therefore it is considered that in America men do
not as in Europe associate daily with those of their
own kindred and neighbourhood only, but with
fellow-creatures from every quarter of the globe; it
will not be thought so surprising that they should
not be so apt to cultivate those amities and chari-
ties which are elsewhere deemed of such moment
to the welfare and comfort of the social life. I remember once to have crossed the Potomac in the
Alexandria ferry-boat with only Mr. Addison and
the two ferry-men. We were only four persons, and
yet it so happened that we were natives of the four
different quarters of the globe. Mr. Addison was
an American, I of Europe, one of the ferry-men an
East Indian, the other an African negro. The coincidence was extraordinary, and it was impossible
not to be struck with it; yet nothing is to be inferred from it. One other such circumstance, and
but another, has befallen me in the course of life.
Alighting in Holborn from a stage-coach, from
Hertfordshire, whither I had been on a visit with
my wife, a fellow-passenger and ourselves sent out
for two hackney-coaches to carry us to our re-
spective homes. Two came, the one No. 1, the
other No. 1000, which are the lowest and the highest numbers. I question whether any other man

has met with anything so extraordinary; yet neither event was in itself of the least consequence, nor at all worthy of regard otherwise than as being very extraordinary.

My public controversy had now attracted some considerable notice in the country; and the Governors of King's College in New York were pleased, unsolicited, to confer on me an honorary degree of Master of Arts, expressly because of the services I had rendered to Church and State. And the troubles of the country growing also every day more serious and alarming, I was very generally applied to by my brethren of the Clergy, chiefly of Virginia, to fall on ways and means of forming something like some general and uniform line of conduct for the whole body of the Clergy of the Church of England throughout the continent. In consequence of this I agreed to accompany, as my neighbour and friend Mr. Addison also did, the Reverend Dr. Cooper, President of King's College in New York, then on a visit to me, to Philadelphia, in his way back to New York. In Philadelphia I spent a week, lodging with Dr. Smith, Provost of the College there; and such a plan was formed and agreed to. It is too well known how little the clergy of Philadelphia regarded this agreement; how generally they went into the views of Congress; and what dreadfully bad consequences this defection of theirs drew after it on the country in general or on the well-affected clergy in particular. Dr. Smith's conduct on the occasion towards me

Some Occurrences noted in my
Passage frm Whaven to Virginia.

Aprl the 27th 1759 Set sail in company wth the Chinwen & Richmond.

May the 19th a most violent Squall
lay to under bare Poles, & in ye morning
of the 20th fell in wth a large Fleet of
upwards of 20 Sail.

— the 26th were frightned by almost
running upon a monstrous large
Grampus.

June the 9th were chac'd by a Vessel
from wd Wve, wth Difficulty escap'd
by Fav.r of the Night.

the 29th being very near Nantucket
saw large Quantities of Grass & Reeds.

the 30th Spoke the Peral Captn Montgomery from London for Virginia.
He had been out 9 weeks & 5 Days, &
reckon'd as well as we in Long. 66.—

July the 5th were brot to by the Kg George
Captn Benjat Hallowell a King's Ship
of 20 Guns from Boston, she reckons
70 Leagues from the Land, & informs us
of five Privateers being upon the
Coast. Ex Quibus, Domine, libera nos!

A PAGE OF JONATHAN BOUCHER'S NOTE-BOOK

was base and false in the extreme; and we have
never since had the least intercourse. I seemed not
much to like either Philadelphia or its inhabitants;
though I received many civilities from them. The
city is disgusting from its uniformity and same-
ness; one street has nothing to distinguish it from
another, but that one is the first, and another the
second, and so on. There are no squares, no public
edifices of any size or dignity; the situation is flat
and level; and, in short, everything about it has a
quakerly or rather, a Republican, aspect.

The people too are like their town, all very well,
but nothing more. One is as good as another, and
no better; and it is in vain to look for anything like
character among them. In one point, not contented with being not agreeable they are almost
disagreeable: the almost universal topic of conversation among them is the superiority of Philadelphia over every other spot of the globe. All their
geese are swans: and it is a fact not to be denied
that by thus for ever trumpeting their own praise
they have in some degree prevailed on their neighbours to acquiesce in their claim to it; just as the
French are supposed to have made all the world
agree in giving the preference to their language.
I used to consider the two colleges of Philadelphia,
and that at Princeton in the Jersies, as the chief
nurseries of all that frivolous and mischievous kind
of knowledge which passed for learning in America.
Like some of the Academies in and around London, they pretended to teach everything, without

being really competent to the teaching of anything
as it ought to have been taught: but their chief and
peculiar merit was thought to be in Rhetoric and
the belles lettres, a term not easily defined nor
understood. Hence in no country were there so
many orators, or so many smatterers. Two or
three years spent at one of these seminaries were
in general deemed sufficient to qualify a person for
the Gown; and persons so qualified had now pretty
generally gotten the churches, which in Virginia
were immediately in the gift of the people; and
even in Maryland the wishes of the people had
great weight with the Governor, who was there the
patron of all church preferments. It is surprising
what improper and indecent contentions these
popular elections occasioned. I have oftener than
once known half-a-dozen candidates all trying for
a vacant parish, and preaching alternately, to give
their electors an opportunity of determining which
they liked best. *Voice and action*, as is remarked
in a very humorous pamphlet respecting London
lectureships, almost constantly carried it. These
frequent appeals and applications to the people, in
this way, as well as from the merchants who meanly
solicited and *begged*, as it was called, consignments
of tobacco, gave them an opinion of their importance and a consequence, unknown to people in
other countries. What influence this had, and how
much it was felt by the friends of Government in
the commotions that now came on, can be known
only to those who were on the spot, who were ob-

servant, and who had some knowledge of the workings of human nature. Preachers and ministers so elected continuing still in some degree dependent on the people, continued also chiefly to cultivate those arts by which their favour had first been gained: their sermons were light, flippant, and ordinary; but their manner of preaching was pleasing and popular. These two Colleges of Princeton and Philadelphia manufactured physicians also with equal facility: I have known many a young man come and set up as a doctor in a neighbourhood in all due form, and with all requisite authority, after a winter or two spent in the *University* of Philadelphia. As for lawyers, they seemed to grow up spontaneously; many of the first name and note in that profession were men without any education and totally illiterate. Such a state of society was peculiar, and could not but have peculiar effects; for no other body of men, nor all the other bodies of men put together, had half so much influence as the lawyers.

I now come to speak of times and events of such magnitude and importance as to have engaged the attention, not of many single individuals only, or many single nations, but of the world, and the effects of which the world is likely long to feel. In the little that I shall have occasion here to say of it I will endeavour to be impartial; I say *endeavour*, because though conscious that I have no by ends to serve by a falsification of truth, and duly confident also in my own integrity that nothing should tempt me knowingly to violate truth, I am exceedingly sensible how difficult it is to come at it. Men so studiously conceal and disguise the true motives of their conduct, and the real and ostensible causes of action are at such variance, and they are moreover oftentimes so very unreasonable, and inconsistent, that when the truth is predicated of them, it actually appears improbable and incredible. It is impossible, moreover, for the most dispassionate man, who feels himself much interested in any controverted question, not to take a part and to feel some bias. On my guard against all such sources of deception and error, I now undertake to speak of the side I took in this great controversy.

Much of what has been already related makes indeed a part of the history of what I did in the revolt. My controversy with Messrs Chase and Paca, my opposition to the strangely wrong and dangerous innovations meditated against Churchmen, and above all, my confidential intimacy with the Governor, were more than sufficient to procure me the honour of being set down as a Government-man. It was an obvious policy in the insurgents to get rid of such men, and accordingly I was soon marked as a man not to be endured.

As I do not propose here to write the history of the revolt, I shall not speak of any Associations, Committees, Military Enrolments, or other manœuvres of the sort, in which I was not myself immediately concerned. I endeavoured in my sermons, and in various pieces published in the Gazettes of the country, to check the immense mischief that was impending, but I endeavoured in vain. I was soon restrained from preaching, and the Press was no longer open to me. The first open and avowed violence I met with was on account of my expressly declining, when applied to by some noisy patriots heretofore of no great note, to preach a sermon to recommend the suffering people of Boston to the charity of my parish. Their port was shut up by Act of Parliament; and as it was alleged that they suffered thus in the common cause, contributions were collected for them all over the continent: the true motive was by these means to raise a sum sufficient to purchase arms and ammunition. I also refused to set my hand to various Associations and Resolves, all, in my estimation, very unnecessary, unwise, and unjust. In consequence of which I soon became a marked man; and though I endeavoured to conduct myself with all possible temper and even caution, I daily met with insults, indignities, and injuries. At length Informations respecting my supposed inimicality to America were regularly sworn to, and laid before the Provincial Committee sitting in Annapolis. My accusers were a Papist and two Presbyterians, one of whom only was my own parishioner. A body of militia was ordered to take me immediately into custody, and accordingly not less than two hundred came to the Governor's, where I then was on a visit, to seize and carry me before the Committee. I had had early and pretty full notice of what was going forward, a circumstance which gave me no common uneasiness. For the charges said to have been brought against me were, as is usual, much exaggerated, and consequently my danger. My friends were alarmed for me, and pressed me so importunately to save myself by flight that I hardly knew how to resist them. My own judgment was strongly against this. I saw, or imagined I saw, from the first that this was the very thing my enemies wished for, and that of course to comply with the advice of my friends would be to fall into the pit my persecutors had dug for me. Yet the Governor, his Council, and a large number of the most respectable persons in the province, were as strongly for my flying as I alone was for my not flying. Luckily the debate was put an end to by the arrival of the armed men, to whom I immediately and resolutely went out; and knowing the captain, I asked what his business with me was. He answered, to carry me before the Committee. When, on my further enquiry, he had told me who were the members of the Committee then sitting, I was not a little surprised to find Messrs Chase and Paca in their number: though I knew they were at the bottom of the mischief, I did suppose they would so far have consulted appearances as not openly to have appeared, with a mob to back them, against a man who was allowed so lately to have given them a complete drubbing when committed together in a fair field. However, making a virtue of necessity, I plucked up courage, and peremptorily told the Captain I would not be carried to this, or any other Committee unknown to the laws, *alive*; but if he would take his men away, I gave him my honour I would, as a gentleman, wait on the gentlemen who composed the Committee: and I desired him with my compliments to deliver this message to the gentlemen assembled for the purpose. The man did as I desired him, and I soon followed him, single, and in high spirits.

As I was going into the Committee Room, and squeezing through an immense crowd, one of the most forward and noted blackguards in Annapolis, then acting as a serjeant in the Militia called together on this occasion, with that kind of generous impatience so common to the Irish (he was an Irishman, a hatter, and of the name of Lindsay) whispered in my ear that he knew I would go on with the same spirit with which I had begun; — and that I might do so, he assured me I had more friends among those who bore arms than enemies, *and by Jasus if he lived he would die with me.* A message in my favour from the Congress itself would not have inspired me with more courage than I felt on this declaration of this honest Teague. When the President was beginning to speak to me I insisted on being permitted first to sit down; and protesting against their having any authority over me, I nevertheless declared that, conscious of my own rectitude of intention, there was nothing which, as gentlemen, they could put to me to which I was not ready, as a gentleman, to give fair, and I hoped satisfactory answers. The charges were now all read in ample form, and a copy of them delivered me; and sundry of the members harangued long and loudly on the danger of such a man's being allowed publicly to avow such principles. It was on this occasion that for the first time in my life I attempted to make a public speech. Necessity may perhaps be the parent of eloquence, as it is said to be of other gifts of genius; and it did indeed once loose the tongue of one who till then had been dumb. It certainly was of great moment to me to say something if it was possible that might make some impression in my favour. What it was that I did say I perhaps could not have told the moment after it was said, and much less now. I remember only that after it was over I reflected on Lord Chesterfield's observation, that the manner of a speech is of much more consequence than the matter. And I remember also that in whatever I said I addressed myself more to the multitude around me than I did to those who were sitting as my judges. In such an emergency this was fair policy, and it had its effect. Many bawled out aloud that what I had said was quite satisfactory, and I was accordingly acquitted.

My thus coming off with flying colours served but to heighten the ill-will of my particular enemies: determined on my ruin, they watched but for an opportunity to effect it. In such times it was little likely such an opportunity should not soon offer.

I happened to be going across the Potomac to Alexandria with my wife and some other of our friends, exactly at the time that General Washington was crossing it on his way to the Northward, whither he was going to take the command of the Continental Army. There had been a great meeting of people, and great doings, in Alexandria on the occasion; and everybody seemed to be on fire, either with rum, or patriotism, or both. Some patriots in our boat huzzaed, and gave three cheers to the General as he passed us; whilst Mr. Addison and myself contented ourselves with pulling off our hats. The General (then only Colonel) Washington beckoned us to stop, as we did, just, as he said, to shake us by the hand. His behaviour to me was now, as it had always been, polite and respectful, and I shall for ever remember what passed in the few disturbed moments of conversation we then had. From his going on the errand he was, I foresaw and apprised him of much that has since happened; in particular that there would certainly then be a civil war, and that the Americans would soon declare for independency. With more earnestness than was usual with his great reserve he scouted my apprehensions, adding (and I believe with perfect sincerity) that if ever I heard of his joining in any such measures I had his leave to set him down for everything wicked. Like Hazael, he might have said, Is thy servant a dog that he should do this great thing? So little do men know of themselves, and so dangerous is it to make one false step.

Many a man, it may be, has gone through life without ever making any egregiously false step; but I question if an instance can be named when a man, having made one false step, made but one. When once a man goes one mile from the strict line of rectitude, he soon sees, or fancies he sees, reasons compelling him to go *twain*. This was the last time I ever saw this gentleman, who, contrary to all reasonable expectation, has since so distinguished himself as that he will probably be handed down to posterity as one of the first characters of the age.

I had some time before this sent to the Virginia Gazette an epigram or two for publication. The printer to whom I entrusted it was, unfortunately for me, then a candidate for the public business; and to curry favour with some of the leading men he shewed my poor epigram, which was instantly voted to be exceedingly obnoxious, and the author of it inimical to America. Among others, he shewed it to a Colonel Carter, who had once been my parishioner and friend, and who declared that the handwriting was mine. It is impossible to conceive what a noise this little squib made in that colony, where I was very generally known: the patriots could not have shewn more resentment had I even framed the Acts of which they so much complained, and which, there is good reason to believe, that old scoundrel Franklin first suggested the idea of, if he did not actually frame them. This Colonel Carter unluckily was in Alexandria on this most unlucky day; and I had not been half an hour there before he found me out, and attacked me on the score of the epigram. A private grudge also brought on me this mischief. The father-in-law of this gentleman had in a strange fit of aristocratic insolence, some time before run his sword through the body of a Mr. Routledge and killed him. For this he was taken up, but bailed in a very extraordinary manner; and in a still more extraordinary manner was found dead, it was never known how, the night before the trial was to come on. During his confinement many papers were published to mitigate or excuse this Colonel Chiswell. Mr. Routledge was an entire stranger to me, though my countryman; but the efforts made in behalf of his murderer were such an outrage on common sense as well as on humanity, that I could not help drawing up some answers to these vindications, which were supposed to have made some impression on the public. *Hinc illæ lachrymæ!*

A mob soon collected around us; and seeing no *Lindsay* among them, but, on the contrary, that they were headed by a very virulent Presbyterian, it soon occurred to me that if I got off at all it must be by stratagem. Accordingly after the first onsets, which were very violent, when I had gotten leave to speak, I again addressed myself, not to my particular opponents, but to the surrounding multitude. And first I excepted against Mr. Ramsay, the Presbyterian, as an improper judge of what was wrong and what was right in a minister of the Church of England, to all of whom he was well known to bear a rooted enmity. I next begged leave to account for Colonel Carter's indignation against me; and so, relating the particulars just set down respecting Colonel Chiswell, I begged them not to suffer themselves to be so duped as to become the tools of a cowardly man who thus sought to revenge his private quarrel. 'I assure you, gentlemen, all this bustle is about a private difference between the Colonel and myself, which I am ready to settle with him this moment, as a man of honour ought to settle private differences.' It would seem that I knew my man: the Colonel complained of my artifice, and declared he would not be my dupe and let me get off so. The people attributed this to his being afraid of me; and so the epigram was dropped, and I again got off.

All this while my poor wife and sister were in an adjoining house, within sight and almost within hearing. What their agitations must have been it is impossible to describe. I promised her that I never would go into Alexandria, nor (if it was possible to avoid it) into any public place again; and I kept my word.

It was proper however and necessary that at least I should continue to go to church. My wife's uncle Mr. Addison's parish was supposed to be somewhat quieter than mine; and as this was the case, and my estate also lay in it, I left Queen Anne and removed to The Lodge, where I officiated as Mr. Addison's curate; having put a Mr. Harrison, brother to the gentleman of that name who was afterwards Mr. Washington's secretary, into the cure of my parish. In the usual and regular course of preaching I happened one Sunday to recommend peaceableness; on which a Mr. Lee and sundry others, supposing my sermon to be what they called a stroke at the times, rose up and left the church. This was a signal to the people to consider every sermon of mine as hostile to the views and interests of America; and accordingly I never after went into a pulpit without something very disagreeable happening. I received sundry messages and letters threatening me with the most fatal consequences if I did not (not desist from preaching at all, but) preach what should be agreeable to the friends of America. All the answer I gave to these threats was in my sermons, in which I uniformly and resolutely declared that I never could suffer any merely human authority to intimidate me from performing what in my conscience I believed and knew to be my duty to God and His Church. And for more than six months I preached, when I did preach, with a pair of loaded pistols lying on the cushion; having given notice that if any man, or body of men, could possibly be so lost to all sense of decency and propriety as to attempt really to do what had been long threatened, that is, to drag me out of my own pulpit, I should think myself justified before God and man in repelling violence by violence.

May 25th

It should have been mentioned long ago that, while I lived at Castle Magruder, some of the patriots of my parish, which swarmed with them, were for ever stirring up anybody they could find at all so disposed, to give me trouble and vexation. They made a great outcry about my refusing to receive some corn I had bought of a planter; notwithstanding that I proved that the corn he offered to deliver me was not marketable. This is mentioned only to shew that among such men in such times it becomes even meritorious to injure and insult an honest man who has had the misfortune to be voted obnoxious. Among others, I fell into a dispute with a blacksmith; the consequences of which, as it happened, did me no little service. He had a cornfield adjoining to my pasture, the fence of which was so bad, that a favourite and valuable horse of mine, though fettered, got over into it. Finding him in his field, this fellow actually shot at him, and lodged several large swan-shot in different parts of his body, so that he was for ever after lame. To aggravate this shocking behaviour still more, it was done in the sight of my wife, and not without much abuse of her husband. And as if he valued himself on his feat, he soon after came swaggering up to me, swore much, and talked much impudent nonsense; adding, whilst his gun was in one hand and a large stick in the other, which he often shook at me, that by G—d he would serve me as he had served my horse. This was too much. I saw it was his plan, if possible, to provoke me to strike him, and to have a trial of strength with me; and being a stoutish fellow, and I utterly unused to boxing, no doubt he counted on gaining a cheap victory, and of course much credit. I desired him repeatedly to keep his distance, instead of which he thrust his fist in my face. No alternative seemed now to be left, and so as we were to come to blows, I determined to have the first. I struck him but once, when 'prostrate he fell, and measured o'er a length of ground.' No man who has never himself experienced such a state of society as then prevailed in that country, can conceive what credit I gained, and, I add, what advantage, from this lucky blow. I was looked upon and spoken of as another Broughton; and it was of more advantage to me to be so thought of than to have been set down as a Newton. In my controversy with Messrs Chase and Paca, some personalities had occurred; and in a controversy when did they not occur? The laugh was turned particularly upon Paca, who, though neither absurd nor ridiculous, was but a weakish man, and exquisitely alive to the state of the public opinion concerning him. In short, he was so hurt as to fancy it incumbent on him to give me a regular and formal challenge; and accordingly applied to my friend Mr. Smith, the secretary to the Governor, to be his second. Mr. Smith with great readiness of mind and adroitness told him that I had foreseen long ago how our dispute would terminate, and accordingly had actually engaged him to attend me as my second on the occasion. This well-timed invention staggered my adversary; which Smith improved by reciting sundry imaginary instances of my astonishing courage and prowess. Thus was I without any plan or wishes of my own all at once set up as a d——d fellow, equally in favour with Mars and Minerva. And I have every reason in the world to believe that this opinion alone saved my bacon on many occasions. One only I will now set down. I dined with Mr. Addison Murdock, a gentleman of considerable respectability, and a near relation of my wife's, in a large company of men of different parties and opinions. Among others was Dr. Brookes, a well-meaning, sensible, but blundering man, and a Mr. Osborne Sprigg, a very great patriot, who had been very busy in the corn story, and who could not forgive me for having defeated him in his attempts to fasten on me suspicions of having done wrong instead of having suffered wrong. Dr. Brookes, with the best intentions I daresay, gave as a toast, 'May the Americans all hang together in accord and concord!' Prompted no doubt by my evil genius, I said, before I well knew what I was saying, 'in any cord, Doctor, so it be but a strong cord.' It was the appearance of wit in this retort, I suppose, which tempted me, and which, after all, I believe may be found in Joe Miller. The patriot took fire immediately; but the explanation I made satisfied everybody else, and things might again have gone on smoothly, had not the wretch, determined to quarrel with me, when his turn came, given as his toast, 'Damnation to General Gage, the troops under his command, and all who wish well to them,' which I refused to drink, as when I did several others also did. Mr. Sprigg now grew outrageous, blustered and threatened at a prodigious rate, and several times pretended to get up to strike me, and seemed to be unwillingly restrained by the company. I sat perfectly still and composed, till at length when there was a little pause, I just said, 'Sir, I believe everybody, as well as myself, has seen that you have determined to quarrel with me; you no doubt thought the opportunity favourable for your purpose; and I have observed you swallow large draughts of wine to render you pot-valiant. But, Sir, I will again disappoint you: permit me, gentlemen, to entreat you only to sit still, and I will stake my life for it, the gentleman will not think of coming near me.' This address had its effect, for he now recollected that bruising was ungentlemanly, and that as I was said to have studied under Broughton, I might possibly be an over-match for him; and therefore I should hear from him next morning *as a gentleman*. I replied, ''Tis very well, Sir: you are no acquaintance of mine; and if those who are your friends think the retreat you are now making a handsome one, I am contented. For the rest, I never did yet hear of your having acted in any instance *as a gentleman*; and if I should to-morrow morning, all I can say is, it will exceedingly surprise me: I shall be at my own home all day.' But I never heard more of him *as a gentle-man*.

It was not on this occasion only that I have ex-perienced that the true way to escape a danger is fairly to meet it. I have, I believe, a tolerably vig-orous and resolute mind; but as to fighting, in every mode of it, there is nothing I so much dread and detest. Everything therefore that I did in that way was really and truly to preserve me from fighting. And it appears that I succeeded.

The principles and ways of thinking of Whigs and Tories, or of Republicans and Loyalists, are hardly more different than are their tempers. The latter have a foolish good-nature and improvidence about them which leads them often to hurt their own interests by promoting those of their adver-saries, when the objects for which they contended are removed; but the former never forgives, never ceases to effect his purposes of being revenged on those he has once called his enemies. Mr. Sprigg was a thorough Whig, and I perhaps as thorough a Loyalist; as appeared on the last fracas of the kind in which I was involved, and which now soon took place.

A public fast was ordained. In America, as in the Grand Rebellion in England, much execution was done by sermons. Those persons who have read any out of the great number of Puritan ser-mons that were then printed as well as preached, will cease to wonder that so many people were worked up into such a state of frenzy; and I who either heard, or heard of, many similar discourses from the pulpits in America, felt the effects of them no less than they had before been felt here. My curate was but a weak brother, yet a strong Republican, i.e. as far as he knew how. The sermon he had preached on a former fast, though very silly, was still more exceptionable as contributing to blow the coals of sedition. Its silliness perhaps made it even more mischievous; for to be very popular, it is, I believe, necessary to be very like the bulk of the people, that is, wrong-headed, ignorant, and prone to resist authority. And I am persuaded, whenever it happens that a really sensible man becomes the idol of the people, it must be owing to his possessing a talent of letting himself down to their level. It remains to be proved, however, that ever a really sensible person did take this part; I think the contrary may be proved. As, however, Mr. Harrison's practice as well as preaching were now beginning to be exceptionable, that is, by his setting about and promoting factious Associations and subscriptions, it was thought necessary that on the approaching fast-day, which was a day of great expectation, I should make a point of appearing in my own pulpit; and the Governor waited on me on purpose to press my doing so.

On my informing Mr. Harrison that this was my intention, he told me he had prepared a sermon for the occasion. I asked him what subject he had pitched upon, and I never shall forget his reply. He proposed, he said, to preach against *absolute monarchy*. It was impossible, I said, not to commend the judiciousness of his choice; as the times and the country in which our lot had fallen so particularly called on us to put our people on their guard against a danger into which they seemed so likely to fall. The fact was, I fancy, he had found such a sermon in Hoadly, and having transcribed it, shewed it to the Committee, by whom it was approved, as any and every thing was and would have been, however loose and weak, that but seemed to be against power and for liberty.

Mr. Addison, the Governor, and all the most judicious friends I had, looked over my sermon, and thought I had softened it down so, as that it might do good, and at least could not possibly give offence. In this and everything else that I now wrote, all that I could dare to hope to effect, was the restraining the body of the people from taking any active part; and the jet of my arguments was that in taking a part they could not be sure they were right and doing good; and so their truest wisdom as well as duty in so difficult a conjecture was, as the Prophet advised them, to *sit still*. And sadly as things went against loyalty and loyal men, I have the comfort to reflect that some good was done by my efforts in their favour. I had some credit and character with my brethren of the clergy, many of whom were thus restrained within the bounds of duty. And as a proof that many of the people were so restrained, I may mention that when members for the Provincial Congress were to be chosen, as the measure was quite novel and altogether unknown to our laws, I exhorted my people to abstain from it, and not one of them attended. Out of the whole county there were but thirteen electors; and in Annapolis there were but four. And it is a certain fact, of the truth of which I at least am thoroughly convinced, that nine out of ten of the people of America, properly so called, were adverse to the revolt. But how shall an historian prove so extraordinary a fact, or expect to gain credit if he should prove it?

When the fast-day came I set off, accompanied by Mr. Walter Dulany, since made a major in a Provincial Loyal Regiment, and was at my church at least a quarter of an hour before the usual time of beginning service. But behold, Mr. Harrison was in the desk, and was expected also, as I was soon told, to preach. This was not agreeable: but of how little significance was this compared to what I next saw, viz. my church filled with not less than 200 armed men, under the command of Mr. Osborne Sprigg, who soon let me know I was not to preach. I returned for answer that the pulpit was my own, and as such I would use it; and that there was but one way by which they could keep me out of it, and that was by taking away my life. In church I managed to place myself so as to have the command of the pulpit, and told my curate at his peril not to attempt to dispossess me. Sundry messages were sent, and applications made to me, to relinquish my purpose; but as I knew it was my

duty, and thought also that it was my interest, not
to relinquish it, I persisted. And so at the proper
time, with my sermon in one hand and a loaded
pistol in the other, like Nehemiah, I prepared to
ascend the steps of the pulpit, when behold, one of
my friends (Mr. David Crawford of Upper Marlborough) having got behind me, threw his arms
around mine and held me fast. He assured me on
his honour he had both seen and heard the most
positive orders given to twenty men picked out
for the purpose to fire on me the moment I got into
the pulpit, which therefore he never would permit
me to do, unless I was stronger than he and two or
three others who stood close to him. I entreated
him and them to go with me into the pulpit, as my
life seemed to myself to depend on my not suffering
these outrageous people to carry their point; and I
suppose we should all be safe while we were all together, for Mr. Crawford and those with him were
rather against than for me in politics. In all these
cases I argued that once to flinch was for ever to
invite danger; and that as I could never be out of
the reach of such men till I was out of the country,
my only policy was, if possible, to intimidate them,
as in some degree I had hitherto done. My well-
wishers however prevailed — by force rather than
by persuasion; and when I was down it is horrid
to recollect what a scene of confusion ensued. A
large party insisted I was right in claiming and
using my own pulpit; but Sprigg and his company
were now grown more violent, and soon managed

so as to surround me, and to exclude every moderate man. Seeing myself thus circumstanced, it occurred to me that things seemed now indeed to be growing alarming, and that there was but one way to save my life. This was by seizing Sprigg, as I immediately did, by the collar, and with my cocked pistol in the other hand, assuring him that if any violence was offered to me I would instantly blow his brains out, as I most certainly would have done. I then told him that if he pleased he might conduct me to my horse, and I would leave them. This he did, and we marched together upwards of a hundred yards, I with one hand fastened in his collar and a pistol in the other, guarded by his whole company, whom he had the meanness to order to play on their drums the Rogues' March all the way we went, which they did. All farther that I could then do was to declare, as loud as I could speak, that he had now proved himself to be a complete coward and scoundrel.

Thus ended this dreadful day, which was a Thursday. On the Sunday following I again went to the same church, was again opposed, though more feebly than before, owing to an idea that I never would think of making another attempt. I preached the same sermon I should have preached on the Thursday, with some comments on the transactions of that day. After sermon, notice having been spread of my being at Church, a larger body assembled, and I found myself again surrounded and hustled. But placing my back against a pillar of the church, and being a little raised, I again began to bawl and to harangue, and again got off; so that this affray ended in a war of words.

These attacks, however, now became so frequent and so furious, and the time, moreover, was coming on fast when if I did not associate, and take the oaths against legal government, I should certainly be proscribed, and, what seemed still worse, not have it in my power to get out of their clutches; for on the 10th of September all farther intercourse with Great Britain was to be stopped; so that I now began to have serious thoughts of making my retreat to England. It was far too plain that such a step could not but be in a manner ruinous to all my interests in America, which were then all the interests I had in the world; but it was alas! still plainer that to stay would too probably be equally fatal to my property and my life, and undoubtedly to my peace. On my mentioning this to my wife, she perfectly concurred in opinion with me, and even pressed me to do what seemed to be absolutely necessary. Our scheme, then, was that she was to remain behind me, and take the best care she could of our estate, in the hope that in half a year or so the storm would blow over, and I might return to her. When I told my near neighbour and dearest friend, Mr. Addison, of the resolution we had taken, he was totally against it; chiefly, I believe, because, as it seemed at first view impossible for him to go with me, he dreaded the being left behind and alone: for tho' in all the hurly-burlys he had thought, and even acted, with me, it happened always to be my lot to stand foremost. On farther consideration, however, and when he saw me determined, he began to change his note, and instead of dissuading me, resolved to go along with me.

Another still more distressing difficulty had also now occurred. My dearest and most excellent wife, on the trial (for I was absent from her almost a week, having gone to Annapolis to settle some businesses of importance, which no person but myself could have settled, and also to take my passage) found that she should never be equal to my leaving her; and so she wrote to me in the most earnest and persuasive manner, entreating me not to argue the point with her, but to comply with her request. Since her death I have found among her few papers the following well-known lines which she had transcribed at the time I am speaking of, and which I now again transcribe from her copy, not without tears:

> 'Did I but purpose to embark with thee
> On the smooth surface of a summer's sea,
> While gentle zephyrs play in prosperous gales,
> And Fortune's favour fills the swelling sails,
> But would forsake the ship and make the shore
> When the winds whistle and the tempests roar?
> No, *Boucher*, no: one sacred oath has tied
> Our loves, one destiny our life shall guide;
> Nor wild nor deep our common way divide.'[1]

On the same scrap of paper are the two following

[1] [From Prior's *Henry and Emma*. Four of these lines are quoted in *Old Mortality* as the motto to chap. x.]

lines, which, tho' I do not now recollect whence they are taken, I easily see why and when they must have been copied:

'He stands, and mocks, unconscious of a shame,
The voice of clamour and the lies of fame.'

It was now finally resolved that Mr. Addison and his younger son, my wife and myself, should sail for England in the Choptank frigate, Captain Richardson; though we had now not a week to prepare ourselves in, and I was still in Annapolis. I did not reach my own home till the Saturday, and on the Sunday morning we were to set off; because if we had not, we were assured that on Monday morning Mr. Sprigg and his myrmidons, who were of what they called *a Committee of Safety*, would wait on us with the new oaths, and proscribe us if we declined to take them. My house was filled with many kind friends who had come to take leave of us; and though my dearest Nelly had got everything ready for our departure more than I had thought it possible she should, so far, I mean, as related to the getting of our stock etc. on board a craft to be carried to the ship, and hiring a schooner to carry us, I had still so much to do that for that night I never went to bed.

Mr. Overton Carr, the son of a very worthy gentleman of Louisa county in Virginia, himself very worthy, and who had long been my pupil, had about six months before married the only sister of my wife; and they continued to live with us. To him I gave a general Power of Attorney; and settled every account I had in the world; wrote down full and very particular directions of everything I wished to have done, respecting every kind of business, during my absence, and made my will. It is of use in such conjunctures to have the mind much employed: the constant agitation in which I had long been kept prevented my feeling so much pain, as if I had had leisure to think of it I certainly should have felt on thus leaving a country, where now almost all my attachments were, to go to another now become foreign to me, where I had no friends, and knew not how to live for even the six months I expected to be absent. Even a little self-delusion on such occasions is not to be discouraged. I wished to believe we should return, and therefore was not too nice in examining how far it was probable or improbable. It seemed, however, to our friends to be of moment to the preservation of our property, that we should go away with the avowed purpose of returning soon; and that we might appear effectually to do so we took none of our effects with us, not even our apparel. I came away with but one suit of clothes, and Bills of Exchange to the amount of a little better than four hundred pounds.

Before I quite close my American history, being now come to the period of my embarkation, it may not be amiss to copy and preserve here two or three papers out of some hundreds which I wrote on the occasion of the troubles, merely to shew how the case appeared at the time to one honest ob-

serving man on the spot; or at least to shew on
what principles, and with what views, my own opposition originated and was conducted.

Quæres addressed to the people of Maryland

1. Do not the popular meetings now so common
among us bear a very near resemblance to the
tribunitial assemblies of the people in the earlier
periods of the Roman history?

2. Do not the resolves entered into at such popular meetings, and framed and supported so as to
have nearly the force of laws, resemble also the
Plebiscita, or *Ordinances*, which in after times were
as valid and obligatory as the Senatus-consulta, or
laws constitutionally enacted by the whole legislature?

3. Should these two quæres be answered in the
affirmative, does it not deserve some consideration, whether by encouraging these, we do not in
fact encourage that Dominatio Plebis, so much
desecrated [*sic*] by the best writers on Government?

4. What good reason can be given for any Committees, not known to the laws of the land or the
Constitution, taking upon them to debate and determine on matters of the highest moment, and
which affect the very vitals of our Constitution?

5. Admitting that their decisions and determina-
tions have been, are, and will be always just and
wise, yet is not their taking upon them, not only
without any authority, but contrary to authority,

the exercise of any such powers, itself a greater grievance than any of those complained of ?

6. Can the Resolves of the General Committee of the several counties of this Province (as published last week in this Gazette) be, with either truth or propriety, said to express the sense of the people of this Province?

7. Did one man in a thousand of the people of this Province give a vote for any of the members of the said General Committee?

8. Has one man in ten thousand of the people of this Province yet expressed his approbation of these Resolves, either himself or by his legal representatives?

9. Are the dissentients among the members of the General Committee to be considered as bound by Resolves against which they actually voted, when a motion for a previous Resolve that the Resolutions of the majority should bind the minority could not be carried?

10. If such members in the Committee declared themselves not bound, with what consistency do they now join with the other members to enforce such Resolves on the people at large by penalties of such cogency and effect as no regular legislature ever ventured to adopt?

11. On what principles either of justice or common sense, or even of the common ideas of liberty, are the people of this Province, or any individuals thereof, to be restrained from debating on and questioning any public measures, where they are not

restrained either by the laws of God or the laws of the land?

12. What is tyranny but the assumption and exercise of power without any authority?

13. What liberty can the people of this Province be said to enjoy, when their arms necessary for their personal defence and support have been arbitrarily taken from them; when they no longer have a free press; when the ministers of the Word of God are dictated to and controlled in their holy function and when even the freedom of private debate is overawed by Committee-censures and the denunciation of tar and feathers?

To the Honble The Deputies in Congress from the Southern Provinces.

GENTLEMEN,

It is some proof of the sad state of the times that we, the writers of this Address, though of some note in our country, and well known to you, find it necessary to communicate our sentiments to you through the medium of a newspaper. Yet conscious that we are not less interested than yourselves in the issue of this unhappy dispute, and conscious also that we have an equal right to debate and determine how it shall be conducted, we claim your attention. And be not so unwise to yourselves and unjust to us as to vote our remarks to be undeserving your notice, merely because owing to the high hand with which a certain party have carried all their points, we convey them to you through a proscribed newspaper, and without the signature of our real names.

Sent originally as ye were to mediate between us and our parent State, even the few who appointed you could and did commission you only to examine into and ascertain our alleged grievances, and to point out the best means of obtaining redress. The single question before you, as a Congress, was, whether the Parliament of Great Britain can constitutionally lay internal taxes on her colonies; and if they cannot, whether the 3d. per lb. duty on tea be a tax or not. You have been pleased very summarily to *Resolve* that they cannot. But we wish to remind you that Resolves are not arguments; and we cannot but think it is assuming somewhat too much of the air and consequence of legal and constitutional Assemblies, thus superciliously to obtrude *Resolves* upon us, without condescending to give us any of the reasons which we are to suppose influenced you to make them. And yet from all we see of these Resolves (of which we claim a right to judge, and to be governed by or not as we think we see reason) we are free to tell you we think them unwise, and also that in their operation they will be ruinous.

This is not said at random. They have already drawn down upon us, or soon will, all the horrors of a Civil War, the evils of which alone infinitely surpass all our other political grievances, even if those were as great as our patriots describe them. And unless you can now, in this your second meeting, have the good sense, the virtue and the fortitude to make Resolves against your former Resolves; or the people in general have the uncommon merit to avow and defend, cost them what it may, their real sentiments as well as their real interests, all that remains for us to do is to protest against your counsels, and to withdraw ourselves if we can out of the reach of their effects.

That the people of America should be severed from Great Britain, even your fellow-Congressionalists from the North will not be hardy enough yet to avow; but that this will certainly follow from the measures you have been induced by them to adopt, is obvious to every man who is permitted yet to think for himself. But consider, we pray you, for a moment in what a case we are likely to be should such an event be permitted for our sins to take place. Wholly unable to defend ourselves, see ye not that after some few years of civil broils all the fair settlements in the middle and southern colonies will be seized on by our more enterprising and restless fellow-colonists of the North? At first and for a while perhaps they may be contented to be the Dutch of America, i.e. to be our carriers and fishmongers; for which no doubt, as their sensible historian has observed, they seem to be destined by their situation, soil, and climate: but had so sagacious an observer foreseen that a time might possibly come when all North America should be independent, he would, it is probable, have added to his other remark, that those his Northern brethren would then become also the Goths and Vandals of America. This is not a chimerical conjecture: the history of mankind proves that it is founded in truth and the nature of things. And should the reflection chance to make any such impression on you, as we humbly think it ought, we entreat you only to remember that you are — *from the Southern Provinces*.

Many of you, if not all, we know were educated in the bosom of the Church of England, and would of course be shocked to think that her generous polity should, for the sake only of a little paltry pre-eminence, and a few noisy huzzas to yourselves, be given up for a wild Republic of mad Independents. Now, have you no suspicions that your fellow-patriots from the North meditate a Reformation, as they call it, in Church as well as in State? They must disregard their own principles, and be inconsistent with themselves, if they do not. If you have not read some recent publications, patronized, if not written, by some leading men among them, which prove that this is at the bottom, and the true and great object of all their present commotions, ye are by no means worthy of your present appointments: and if, having read them, ye still remain unconvinced or unconcerned, what shall we say but that ye are still more unworthy? It should not be thought necessary to inform you that Republicanism will but ill accord with the genius of the people whom ye say ye represent. Taught by our fathers and by all our history to love and reverence the Constitution both in Church and State, under which they and we have hitherto happily lived and flourished, be not, we beg leave to entreat you, so fascinated by New England politics as to vote for destroying it, without first well knowing what we are to have in its stead. If you do, we trust your countrymen in general never will. O 'tis a monstrous and an unnatural coalition; and we should as soon expect to see the greatest contrarieties in Nature to meet in harmony, and the wolf and the lamb to feed together, as Virginians to form a cordial union with the saints of New England.

We charge you then, as ye will answer it to your own consciences, and to Him who is the discerner of Consciences, to be on your guard how ye countenance any measures which may eventually lead, first to a separation from Great Britain, and afterwards to the subjugating these Southern colonies to those of the North. Common prudence recommends this caution, no less than common gratitude. Why should we tell you in what a forlorn and helpless plight we are, even amidst all this parade of military preparations, and how utterly unfit to meet in war one of the most powerful nations now upon earth? However convenient it may be to our self-dubbed patriots to conceal the nakedness of our land, it cannot be unknown either to you or us. Exceedingly different from the Northern colonies, we have within ourselves an enemy fully equal to all our strength. From this enemy that no insurrection has yet been raised, we should be thankful to the mild, quiet, and submissive spirits of the numerous body of people alluded to; thankful to the energy still left to our laws; thankful in no small degree to a good and a gracious King, who, were he, like ourselves, to take Cromwell's unhallowed politics for his pattern, might soon find very different employment for our cockaded gentry than that of insulting and ill-treating, as they are now permitted daily to do, unoffending and peaceful citizens; and above all thankful to a good Providence for hitherto preserving us from this most dreadful calamity. We have too an injured, a vindictive and a barbarian enemy on our frontiers who, on the slightest encouragement, would soon glut their savage passion for revenge by desolating our out-lying settlements. How easy will it be for Great Britain, should we so far provoke her, or in her own self-defence, by means of the navigation of the Mississippi to supply them with arms, ammunition, and officers: and how without arms or ammunition for a single campaign, without discipline, officers, or pay, should we be prepared to repel their incursions?

These are but a few of the evils we foresee should we of these Southern provinces continue to give any longer any countenance to the infuriate politics of the Republicans of the North. Even these however we think should be sufficient to deter and determine you. If unhappily for yourselves and us you continue to think otherwise, let personal considerations have their due weight with you. Know ye not on what a perilous precipice ye stand? The single hope on which your all rests is that ye will be supported by the populace, who, we need not tell you, are even proverbially fickle and false. But ye also know that at present whatever your hazardous situation may oblige you to pretend, ye have not the voice of the people with you. It is not indeed yet declared aloud against you; but a very uncommon train of circumstances must concur in your favour, or it soon will. And if ye now fall disgraced, do us the justice to remember that ye will not fall unwarned of your danger.

We have the honour to be etc., etc.

published in Riv-ington's New York Gazette } A large majority of the people of Virginia and Maryland who have any property, and are not in debt.

Copy of a letter to Col. Geo: Washington.

The Lodge, Augt. 6th, 1775

DEAR SIR,

I thought it far from the least pleasing circumstance attending my removal hither that it placed me in your immediate neighbourhood. For having now been happy in your acquaintance several years I could not help considering myself, nor indeed help hoping that I was considered by you, as an old friend; and of course I counted on our living together in the pleasing intercourse of giving and receiving the mutual good offices of neighbourhood and friendship.

That things have turned out much otherwise I need not inform you. Mortified and grieved as I confess myself to be at this disappointment, I am by no means prepared to say that you are wholly to be blamed for it; nor, as I would fain hope you in your turn will own, is it entirely owing to any fault of mine. I can easily suppose at least that we, neither of us, think ourselves to blame: and yet I cannot help thinking that had I been in your place, I should, in this as well as in other things, have taken a different part from that which you have chosen. Permit me, Sir, as one who was once your friend, and at any rate as one not likely to be soon troublesome to you again in the same way, once more as a friend freely to expostulate with you. If I am still in the wrong, I am about to suffer such punishment as might satisfy the malice of even the most vindictive enemy; and if you are wrong as in some degree I think you are, it is my duty frankly to tell you so, and yours to listen to me with patience.

On the great points so long and so fruitlessly debated between us it is not my design now again to solicit your attention. We have now each of us taken and avowed our side, and with such ardour as becomes men who feel themselves to be in earnest in their convictions. That we should both be in the right is impossible, but that we both think we are we must in common candour allow. And

this extreme difference of opinion between ourselves, where we have no grounds for charging each
other with being influenced by any sinister or unworthy motives, should teach us no less candour in
judging of and dealing by others in a similar pre-
dicament. There cannot be anything named of
which I am more strongly convinced, than I am
that all those who with you are promoting the
present apparently popular measures are the true
enemies of their country. This persuasion however
will by no means justify me, should I be so weak
and wicked as to molest them while they do not
molest me. I do not say this because I happen to be
in what is called the minority, and therefore without any power of acting otherwise; it is the decision
of truth and justice, and cannot be violated without doing violence to every system of ethics yet
received in any civilized country. The true plan in
such cases is for each party to defend his own side
as well as he can by fair argument, and also, if possible, to convince his adversary: but everything
that savours of, or but approaches to, coercion or
compulsion is persecution and tyranny.

It is on this ground that I complain of you and
those with whom you side. How large a propor-
tion of the people in general think with you or
think with me it is in none of our powers to ascertain. I believe, because I think I can prove it, that
your party to serve an obvious party purpose exceedingly magnify the numbers of those whom
they suppose to take part with you; and you tax us

with doing the same. But there is this great, manifest, and undisputed difference between us. No Tory has yet in a single instance misused or injured a Whig merely for being a Whig. And whatever may be the boasted superiority of your party, it will not be denied that in some instances at least this has been in our power. With respect to Whigs however, the case has been directly the reverse: a Tory at all in the power of a Whig never escapes ill treatment merely because of his being a Tory. How contrary all this is to all that liberty which Whigs for ever are so forward to profess, needs not be insisted on: it is so contrary to all justice and honour, that were there no other reasons to determine me against it, as there are thousands, I would not be a Whig, because their principles, at least as I see them exemplified in practice, lead so directly to all that is mean and unmanly.

It is a general fault in controversial writers to charge all the errors of a party on every individual of that party. I wish to avoid the disgrace of so indiscriminate a judgment; and therefore have a pleasure in acknowledging that I know many Whigs who are not tyrants. In this number it is but doing you common justice to place you. I wish I could go on, and with equal truth declare, that whilst you forbear yourself to persecute your fellow-subjects on the score of their political creeds, you had been as careful to discourage such persecution in others. Scorning to flatter, as much as I scorn to tax you wrongfully, I am bold thus openly to tell you I think you have much to answer for in this way. It is not a little that you have to answer for with respect to myself.

You know and have acknowledged the sincerity and the purity of my principles; and have been so candid as to lament that you could not think on the great points that now agitate our common country as I do. Now, Sir, it is impossible I should sometimes avow one kind of principles and sometimes another. I have at least the merit of consistency; and neither in any private or public conversation, in anything I have written, nor in anything I have delivered from the pulpit, have I ever asserted any other opinions or doctrines than you have repeatedly heard me assert both in my own house and yours. You cannot say that I deserved to be run down, vilified, and injured in the manner which you know has fallen to my lot, merely because I cannot bring myself to think on some political points just as you and your party would have me think. And yet you have borne to look on, at least as an unconcerned spectator, if not an abettor, whilst like the poor frogs in the fable, I have in a manner been petted to death. I do not ask if such conduct in you was friendly: was it either just, manly, or generous? It was not: no, it was acting with all the base malignity of a virulent Whig. As such, Sir, I resent it: and oppressed and overborne as I may seem to be by popular obloquy, I will not be so wanting in justice to myself as not to tell you, as I now do with honest boldness, that I despise the man who, for any motives, could be induced to act so mean a part. You are no longer worthy of my friendship; a man of honour can no longer without dishonour be connected with you. With your Cause I renounce you; and now, for the last time, subscribe myself, Sir,

Your humble servant

J. B.

On the 10th of September, 1775, in company with Mr. Addison and his younger son, and a Mr. Braithwaite from Annapolis (attended also to the ship by my wife's younger brother and my sister) we left The Lodge, amidst the tears and cries of our slaves, and went on board a small schooner called the Nell Gwyn. Our accommodations here were but bad, and such, as I told my poor wife, as were, I feared, too ominous of the hardships she was about to encounter. She and I slept, I remember, on one of the miserable bunkers in the miserable cabin, with a piece of an old sail for our coverlid, and a small bag of homony for our pillow. Yet she declared she slept soundly, and so did I, owing no doubt to the great exertions both of body and mind to which we had been so long subjected, and by which nature was almost exhausted. After a day and a night spent in this vessel we reached our destined ship, the Choptank frigate, then lying off Quantico. Here we stayed one day; and nothing material happened to us, save that here our two friends, Jack Addison and my sister, took their leave of us. At the mouth of the Potomac we stayed several days, and went often ashore, and were hospitably and genteelly entertained by Mr. Wolstenholme. At length the wind came fair, and we sailed with a fine fresh breeze down the Chesapeak; and on the 20th of the month, just about sunset, in a charmingly fine evening, we lost sight of the capes of Virginia, never to see them more.

To a contemplative mind there certainly is something grand and dignified in a long sea-voyage. The magnificence of Nature is at least seen in a new point of view. I entered on this voyage with such a tone of spirits as I had never before experienced. The part I had acted in the awful confusions on which I had just turned my back was such as I could reflect on with some satisfaction: the part my dear wife, who was natural'y timid even beyond what is usual in her sex, took, was magnanimous, and endeared her to me beyond what I had conceived to be possible. For no bond of attachment, no ties of affection, are so strong as those which are formed by suffering together. And this her extraordinary courage continued not only through the voyage, but in all the subsequent great and hard trials which it was her hard lot to be afterwards called to undergo. It is in little things only that women are cowardly: in great efforts their spirit is not inferior to our own; and in the patient endurance of evils, such as long and severe sicknesses, I am convinced they far excel us in fortitude.

Our voyage was a tempestuous one, but short. My wife kept up her health and spirits astonishingly; but I had the misfortune to be afflicted with a severe bilious fever, from which it was thought I was sometimes in much danger; and I had hardly got tolerably well when on the 20th of October, about mid-day, in fine weather, we landed at Dover.

The verdure of the country even at that season struck and charmed us all; and it would not be easy to give a person who has not either been long absent from such scenes, or in a situation never to have seen them, any adequate idea of the ardour and the rapture with which we viewed the castle and the cliffs at Dover. But when in a day or two afterwards I carried my poor wife into the Cathedral at Canterbury, whilst the organ was playing and the choristers singing, I really doubted, as well as she did, whether it would not have proved too much for her nature to bear. The magnificence of the building, the venerableness of its history, much of which she had read and recollected, and the solemnity of the worship, all so new to her, all conspired to fill her mind with such rapturous sensations, as she had thought it was impossible to have been excited by anything upon earth.

Of her surprise at first seeing London, and her desiring me the first time she was with me in the streets to stop till the crowd should be gone past, I forbear to remark, because such ideas, I presume, may have occurred to others in a similar situation.

We took lodgings all together in Queen's Square, Westminster, at a Mrs. Brookes's, with whose son we had been well acquainted in Annapolis. All that happened of any moment during our short stay here was my obtaining recommendations to Lord Dartmouth and the then Bishop of London, by both of whom I was encouraged to hope something might be done for me. I was weak enough to cherish these hopes for years to no purpose; and I might, if I pleased, fill the remainder of my volume with an account of the various plans and projects I formed by means of various acquaintances and connections I was at infinite pains to form with men of rank and in power, not all of them romantic and unreasonable, but which however all came to nothing. During this period I was a great newspaper writer, and wrote many pieces, some of which were much taken notice of. They were printed chiefly in the Public Advertiser, then one of the most reputable papers; and I received from the Treasury, by means of Mr. Pownall, twice, a gratuity, each time of forty pounds. Soon after in common with loyalists in general, I obtained a regular pension. Mine was at first one hundred pounds a year.

In February 1776 the curacy of Paddington becoming vacant by the resignation of my friend Dr. Myles Cooper in my favour, I removed thither; and we first took lodgings at one Leigh's, a tailor, in Bell Lane, a good house. Here we continued till Midsummer, when both Mr. Addison and his son left us, the former to go on a little tour of pleasure into the country, and the latter to the Academy in Soho Square. Soon after we took a whole house in Paddington to ourselves, at twenty pounds a year. It was unfurnished, and we instantly set about furnishing it in the cheapest way we could, by attending sales, and dealing with brokers etc. To do this took every farthing of money I then had, which was seventy-five pounds. But I had my pension to live on, and the curacy, which was then about sixty pounds a year; but I afterwards raised it to upwards of one hundred pounds a year.

[Two leaves of the original manuscript torn out here.] only *succedaneum* to it within her reach, the intoxicating fervours of enthusiasm. She attended the Methodists for months with all the constancy and zeal in her power, and with a resolution to give up the reins entirely to her imagination. And I have heard her a thousand times complain of the refractoriness of her reason, which, with all the pains she took, she never could so far get the better of as that she could find any gratification, as she saw so many others do, in the mummeries of those religionists.

On leaving Mrs. Hussey's, we took another house in Paddington, of Mr. Hesse, called the Hermitage, for forty pounds a year. The plan of life which I now resolved to pursue was to take a select number of young gentlemen into my house to educate. There was no little likelihood of our being able soon to return to America, from whence I

neither had yet received, nor expected soon to receive, any remittances: and (excepting that I had
now got forty pounds a year more for reading prayers every Sunday, between my own two services in
the church, to the Honourable Mrs. Trevor in Cur-
zon Street), had I yet much bettered my income, or
had any prospects of bettering it: and we neither of
us had yet learned to live on a little. The plan
above mentioned, if it could be affected, was certainly by far the most rational of anything likely
to occur. But without money, connections, or
friends, and more especially without learning, and
with so many competitors all round me, all possessed of all these advantages and many more, it
seemed little less than madness in me to hope for
success.

Yet this hope I did entertain, and I was encouraged to entertain it, chiefly by the suggestions of
the most temperate, judicious, cordial, and valuable
friend that ever any man was blessed with. I here
mean William Stevens Esq: with whom, prompted
by a kind of instinctive congeniality of temper and
principles, I had happily become acquainted without any introduction, soon after our coming to
England, and whose friendship has been, and con-
tinues to be, one of the prime blessings of my life.
Mr. Stevens, though he has spent his life in business, is not only pious and charitable to an uncommon degree, but also a man of very considerable
learning, and one of the ablest divines I am acquainted with. He brought me acquainted with

the present excellent Dean of Canterbury, John Frere Esq: the Reverend Mr. Jones, and Dr. Glasse; whose countenance and encouragement have been to me in lieu of all other patronage.

For some time after we went to the Hermitage, having no boys, more room in our house than we wanted, and more rent to pay than suited our circumstances, we received Mrs. Willis and her daughter as lodgers; and they were our inmates for about three months. This laid the foundation of a most intimate and cordial friendship, which has subsisted between us ever since, and will subsist till it is dissolved by death. Mrs. Willis is in every point of view as amiable and worthy a woman as lives; and she is rendered, if possible, more amiable and dear to me from the circumstance of her having been uncommonly unfortunate.

She is a native of Antigua; but was brought up from her earliest years, and has ever since resided, in England. Being an heiress, handsome, sensible, and agreeable, no wonder she was much courted; but being of an independent mind, and greatly above all mean notions, she resolved to marry for love, in the hope of strongly attaching to her a man of sense and worth, by rendering such an one independent and happy. With this view she married a Mr. Willis, a handsome, sensible man, but with no fortune, and of no family. That fine plans in theory turn out very different when reduced to practice is no new observation. Mr. Willis, intoxicated as it would seem with his sudden elevation, and flattered by the compliments paid to his person, became a man of pleasure, and by a natural progress dissipated, extravagant, licentious and wicked. And so, after living together about twenty years, with a constitution much impaired, and his fortune shattered, he closed the scene in a way not very uncommon with men of pleasure, by a pistol.

His widow had still a noble fortune left, and two sons and a daughter. The two sons she brought up, both of them, at Eton school, which they both went through with great credit; then removed to University College, Oxon, and then to Lincoln's Inn. They both had the reputation of being excellent scholars, and excellent young men of the fairest hopes, and both died of the same disease, viz. a consumption, before they reached their twenty-sixth year. The last and youngest had gone to the West Indies, in hopes of receiving benefit in his malady from the warmth and salubrity of the air there: and his unhappy mother heard the news of his dying at sea, on his return to die, as he fondly hoped, in her bosom, whilst she was with us. It is impossible I should ever forget how affecting our interview was when I was forced to communicate the sad tidings to her.

My friend the late Governor of Maryland, now Sir Robert Eden, unable to stem the torrent of the popular fury any longer, driven from his Government, had now been some time in England, and was ready to send his younger son to me as a pupil whenever I chose to receive him. This was not before another pupil offered, who was a son of Mr. Glassford of Glasgow, one of the most eminent and respectable merchants of his day.

Mr. Glassford was naturally a man of a most liberal turn of mind, and from a sense of duty as well as affection was desirous to spare no expense in doing justice to his son in his education. He had for some time been in the College of Glasgow, but though he was there regarded as already a good scholar, still it was judged necessary to give him a sort of finishing in England. Diffident of his own judgment on such a point, Mr. Glassford had brought up with him his son's quondam tutor, Mr. Young, Greek professor in the College of Glasgow, for the express purpose of choosing and fixing on a proper tutor in England. After looking all around him, and making all the necessary enquiries, Mr. Young at length fixed on Dr. Glasse: but Dr. Glasse, on their applying to him, was full; and therefore very obligingly by Mr. Stevens's instigation, recommended me.

Even his recommendation however was not thought sufficient, till Mr. Young should have an opportunity of forming his own judgment from his own observations. Aware of all this, I was introduced to him on purpose that he might sift and try me.

As I can hardly suppose that any other man was ever circumstanced exactly as I was on this occasion, I can hardly suppose it possible for any man to conceive what my feelings then were. It has

already been noted how totally and miserably un-
learned I was on my first setting out in the world:
and the kind of life I had led in America was such
an one as had neither furnished me with opportunities nor motives to acquire learning. It has,
however, been through life a kind of maxim with
me that I could do anything which I strenuously
resolved to do; and therefore having now once
more resolved to be a schoolmaster, and in a way
very different from what had been the case beyond
the Atlantic, that required real and great abilities,
I resolved to qualify myself for it by hard study.
And no man, I believe, ever studied more intensely
than I now did for some years. It seemed particularly unfortunate and alarming that in the case of
Mr. Glassford's son, the greatest stress was to be
laid on great ability in Greek; where, as ill luck
would have it, I, who was strong in nothing, was
particularly weak. It is a fact at which at this
moment I myself stand astonished, that at the time
I am speaking of I actually hardly knew the Greek
alphabet, and could not have construed a single
line in any Greek author without the Latin version.
Thus and no better qualified, I met Mr. Young,
with whom, as an obvious piece of policy, I took the
lead in conversation, and talked so confidently, if
not plausibly, on various points of Grecian literature, that his report of me was favourable beyond
my most sanguine wishes. Mr. Glassford, besides
a handsome entrance, paid me a first quarter by
way of advance; and his son continued with me

two or three years with great mutual satisfaction, until by teaching him I myself became somewhat of a tolerable Greek scholar, and he left me with the reputation of being a very able one. After him I had a boy of good connections from the West Indies, for whom however I have never to this day been fully paid. And in about a year or so the Earl of Galloway, after various minute enquiries, and in particular after writing to the late Bishop of London (Bishop Lowth) for an opinion of me, who was pleased to express himself very warmly and much in my favour, sent his eldest son to my care, Lord Gairlies: and this so fixed and established me that ever after I had as many boys, all such as one would wish to have, and my house full enough, as long as I continued in the employment. When it was known that so undoubtedly learned and excellent a man as Bishop Lowth had spoken in my favour (and the Earl of Galloway, to justify, I suppose, the removing his son from Westminster school, soon made it very generally known) I no longer wanted any other recommendations. Chance and good fortune, or (as both gratitude and truth should rather have led me to say) the good Providence of God, were thus favourable to me on my setting out; and I was careful not to forfeit them by any negligence or misconduct of my own. For, far enough from being really learned as I always have been, and still am, I yet must be permitted to think, without any vanity, that I was not a bad schoolmaster. I was much in earnest, and I also acted under a constant sense of duty. My dear wife, moreover, acquitted herself of her no less arduous task with uncommon merit. She was a gentlewoman in principle, and so was very far above acting on the mean and mercenary plans which are too often followed by persons in those employments. And easily as the world is cajoled by charlatans, in that line of life more especially, such merits, when once well established, seldom fail in the long run of meeting with its [*sic*] due reward.

Much about this time i.e. in 1779, I had the farther good fortune to be appointed Assistant Secretary to the Society for the Propagation of the Gospel in Foreign Parts, with a salary at first of one hundred pounds a year, but which was afterwards reduced to eighty pounds. My good friend, Mr. Stevens, first put me upon applying for this also; and Archbishop Cornwallis, on the recommendation of Bishop Lowth, was pleased to recommend me to the Society at large, when though there were two or three other candidates, I was chosen with an entire unanimity. The duties of this appointment required some abilities and more labour; but it was reputable, and brought me acquainted with many respectable persons; so that, though at the desire of the present Archbishop of Canterbury, I was induced to resign it, I look back on my connection with that Society, of which I long have been and still am a member, not without much satisfaction.

In 1779 also I had the great good fortune to become acquainted with Miss Barton, which, as it laid the foundation of a very momentous event in the history of my life, I must endeavour to recollect and set down with particular exactness.

She was the elder of two daughters, the only living children of Mr. John Barton, a silk-mercer on Ludgate Hill. Her mother was of the respectable family of the Eyres of Winchester. The two sisters had for some time jointly kept house together in Queen's Square, Bloomsbury: but being of very different tempers, they had parted, and the younger sister then lived in lodgings in Chelsea, where in May, 1780, she died; and her sister inherited all she had. An old servant of the name of Kirsupp, who had lived with the family forty years, had a widow sister in Paddington with whom she lived. Though in a low station and circumstances I never knew a person so little tinctured with vulgar sentiments and manners. She really was a sensible and agreeable as well as very pious old woman; and I cannot but highly respect her memory. Owing to some of those causes which so often baffle all human skill to discover, when she was not far short of seventy years of age, without any known misfortune or calamity, without any apparent disease, she suddenly lost her understanding. During this severe visitation Miss Barton often visited her; and at length the poor old woman's daughter and sister, either tired out with their attendance on her, or too eager to seize the little property, which by the bounty of the Barton family she had to live on, determined to send her to a mad-house, and due authority for the purpose was duly obtained from the proper physicians. This Miss Barton thought too severe a remedy, and endeavoured to prevent it, but endeavoured in vain till, though then we were total strangers to each other, she called on me for aid. I compromised the matter by proposing that Miss Barton alone should be at all the extra expense attending her taking a more private lodging, and managing the poor old woman in her own way. Such a lodging was accordingly taken at Kensington Gravel Pits, where they remained three or four months; where also I was frequently called in; and where finally Miss Barton watched her patient with such unwearied and proper assiduity that there actually, contrary to all reasonable expectation, soon appeared hopes of her recovery; and in about a year she did entirely recover, and ever after continued perfectly well, till she died three or four years afterwards.

Miss Barton had now become so attached to Paddington, and took such an interest in her old servant's being and remaining well, that with my assistance she took and furnished a handsome house on the Green, where Kirsup lived with her.

To understand my story here, it is necessary I should give some more particular account of Miss Barton, whose character, though worthy and amiable in the extreme, was certainly peculiar, and in some respects extraordinary. But here I feel myself much at a loss how to proceed. I lie under such great and uncommon obligations to this excellent woman that I can hardly help feeling it as too near an approach to ingratitude to set down sundry little peculiarities, which yet I must set down, or do violence to truth and consistency. She had been well educated, was extremely religious, well-informed, and sensible; but she had a natural restlessness of mind about her which seemed constitutional, and which therefore it seemed impossible to quiet. She was for ever haunted with dismal apprehensions: yet she was by no means unreasonably attached to the good things of this world, nor was she at all tinctured with any religious despondencies, the two subjects which most usually, I think, engage such unhappy minds. She was however pretty generally fidgetting, restless, uneasy, and unhappy about something or other; which she was at so little pains to suppress or conceal, that not a few superficial observers hastily ascribed so striking a peculiarity of manner to an actual derangement of mind. This however was really no more her unhappy case than it is with everybody else who in any instance thinks and acts unreasonably. She had upon the whole a better cultivated and a better regulated understanding than falls to the lot of nine women in ten: though I readily acknowledge that, according to a phrase of her own, in a thousand instances she was *odd;* and both thought and acted in such a way, daily, and on many occasions, as it was hardly possible rationally to account for.

The younger sister had a busy projecting head: and so, dissatisfied with an income of two hundred pounds a year, which she thought scanty, she had fallen upon various schemes to augment it, and particularly on that of buying annuities. This had naturally brought her connected with sundry necessitous sharp adventurers, with whom of course, on some account or other, she was for ever involved in some trouble or other. This property with these appendages her sister inherited: and indeed her own fortune was by no means pleasantly circumstanced, a very large part of it being either lent to, or somehow or other in the hands of attorneys.

She had no nearer relation than a Mr. Barnard, an attorney-at-law, living in Bartlett's Buildings, Holborn; and he was only a third or fourth cousin; and a person for whom moreover she had not the least esteem or regard. This gentleman had been employed by her mother in collecting the outstanding debts, putting out the money, and, in short, in doing all the business of the family that fell in the way of his profession. He had naturally a dull, perplexed and confused understanding, which was however rendered still more confused by his professional habits; for besides this natural obliquity of understanding, he had gotten a way of involving everything that he had the management of in doubts and difficulties; and, in short, entangling and puzzling the plainest things in such a manner that none but a lawyer could disentangle them. Miss Barton always suspected, and I am afraid not without reason, that he was prompted to this kind of conduct not a little by knavery. It unavoidably kept her affairs always in his hands, and so gave him some influence both over her fortune and herself; the former of which it was very obvious he counted confidently on making his own at her death. These things kept her mind in a state of constant fretting and agitation; which was so manifest, that she was aware some people must needs think her hardly compos mentis. Indeed she was thoroughly persuaded that it was one great object with Mr. Barnard if possible to drive her to madness; that so by a statute of lunacy he might sooner come into the possession of her fortune than he could hope to do by waiting for her death. And shocking as such a scheme, so deliberately formed and pursued, must be thought by every really honest man, I am very far from being sure that she suspected him of it wrongfully.

So circumstanced, it was natural, when I had become well acquainted with her, that she should often [A leaf of the original manuscript cut out here.]

Before we set out for Bristol she made her will, written entirely with her own hand from a form with which she was furnished by Messrs W. and I. Lyon of Gray's Inn, and made it entirely in my favour. From the Wells she received little or no benefit, and perceiving her end to be fast drawing nigh, she was eager to return to her own home, as we did in somewhat less than a month. After this she was seldom able to go out at all, or to do anything, but lingered on, happily without any excruciating pains, or anything very distressing, save an extreme shortness of breath occasioned by a pectoral dropsy, till the last day of March, being Easter Sunday, in the night, she died a few minutes only after she had seen and spoken to me with all possible calmness and composure.

I was now legally possessed of property worth not less than five hundred pounds a year; and I hope I neither received, nor have since enjoyed this great acquisition without feeling, if not expressing, due returns of gratitude to the donor; and still more especially without thanking Him my supreme benefactor, from whom cometh every good and perfect gift. Even this blessing however, like all others, I believe, that are merely human, I was not to be permitted to enjoy without some alloy and some drawbacks. Mr. Barnard, as might have been foreseen, though I did not foresee it, was grievously disappointed and chagrined, for I acted by him with more openness than [some lines missing] him an opportunity of entering a Caveat [a few words missing] plagued me for upwards of a year; and though at last I happily got the better of him, it cost me seven or eight hundred pounds first in law.

I have forgotten to relate in its place an incident which occurred whilst we were at the Hot Wells, on which I often reflect, not, I own, without much satisfaction. The maid of the house where we lodged was a native of the village of Long Aston close by Bristol. Visiting her parents whilst we were there, she happened in the hearing of an old woman their neighbour to mention my name; on which the old woman eagerly laid hold; and finding on farther enquiry that I had been in America, she said I must be that good man who so long ago had been so good there to her dear son.

Next morning she waited on me with her son's letter, which brought the whole transaction back to my memory, and which I will now briefly relate.

Whilst I was Rector of Annapolis, the carpenter of a Bristol ship bound up the bay to Baltimore was put ashore sick at Annapolis. I was sent to, as a clergyman; and finding the poor young fellow in mortification, I thought it my duty to apprise him of his danger; which notice he heard with most uncommon fortitude. He said that, though young, and in a good way of life as he was, it could not but be a desirable thing to him to live, yet as it pleased God to order it otherwise, he was not afraid to die. With the very few things that troubled his mind he would, if I would give him leave, acquaint me. Just before his sailing he had, contrary to the desire of his mother, married a girl in a low sphere of life, and whom he supposed he had left with child. He wished he could have been blessed with his parent's forgiveness before he died; but since that could not be, he begged leave to entreat me to write to

her, to say that on his dying bed he implored her
pardon, and that she would also forgive his poor
forlorn partner, and give to her child, if she had
one by him, what was intended for him. This I
promised him I would do, and I did do it. He then
farther requested me to promise him Christian
burial, a winding-sheet, and a coffin; for his money
was all exhausted, and the captain withheld his
wages on account of his long ill health. These I
also promised and performed. This poor fellow
(John Hayward by name) died like a hero; I add,
like a Christian hero; but not before he had himself, notwithstanding his great weakness, made
shift to write a letter to his poor mother, such an
one as, in my mind, would have done honour to
Cicero, and in which all that, when I afterwards
saw it at Bristol, I could except against, were some
exaggerated expressions of gratitude to me. I saw
him within a few moments of his death, when his
eyes were actually closed, and he unable to open
them. Lifting up one of his eyelids, and squeezing
his clay-cold hand, I desired him to shew me, by
some means or other, whether he recognised me
or not. 'O, I know you well: God bless you! receive the last prayers of a dying man! God bless
you!' His last breath was spent in uttering these
words. Is it to be wondered at that I still strongly
remember such a man and such a scene? When
Miss Barton, in the accidental way that has just
been related, heard the story, she remarked that
she was now at least confirmed beyond a possibility

of wavering in her intentions towards me. This is another instance of the kind dispensations of Providence, which so often brings things about so, as that though a man 'casts his bread on the waters, yet after many days he shall find it again.'

My little seminary of learning seemed all this while, greatly owing to the great worth of my wife, to go on, and to improve and flourish. I kept up my numbers pretty constantly at between twelve and sixteen; and besides the different masters I occasionally employed in different branches of education, I had two constant ushers. Fond as, from principle, temper, and habit, I really am of a life of exertion and application, I should now have had little left to wish for in this world, had not God seen fit that my poor wife, always failing and sickly, should now be overtaken by a complaint that was very alarming. Dr. I. C. Smythe who attended her soon pronounced that all her ailments proceeded from the ossifying of some of the vessels that lead to and from the heart; which lying beyond the reach of medicine, was consequently beyond the reach of cure. Yet as there was nothing imminently mortal in the case, it was possible life might be protracted for years, never indeed with anything like confirmed health, yet not without comfort.

This passing of sentence upon her she insisted on hearing, and did hear it with the most perfect composure; being grieved and loath to die only because she was loath to leave me. On me, when I had time to think of and to weigh it coolly, it had a different effect. From this time I thought only of ways and means not only how to prolong her life, but to prolong it comfortably.

Mr. John James (the second son of my ever honoured friend at Arthuret who had now taken a Doctor's degree, and was become Dr. James) had about this time just gone through his education at Oxford. He was not only one of the best scholars I ever knew, but one of the most sensible and worthy men; and had he been a child of my own I could hardly have loved him more than I did. It was now time to think of his doing something for himself in the world; and his father, who by this time had come to have a little better opinion of my management, desired very much to be governed by my advice. On all these accounts I was led to form a deep scheme to introduce him into my own way of life, now become not only reputable but lucrative; and, in short, to bring matters round so as that I might give up the business and he succeed me in it.

With this view, happening to have it in my power, I rented the house adjoining to the Hermitage, and began to repair and adapt [it] to my purpose; which at length I effected, though at an expense of not less than six hundred pounds. Into this house when finished we withdrew with as many of the boys as could not well be accommodated in the other; Mr. James now acting under me as my assistant. And as he was engaged to an amiable young lady of Carlisle of the name of Hodgson, our plan was that at a proper season he was to marry her, come into the Hermitage, become my partner, and so gradually come into the whole business.

To settle a scheme of this sort, confessedly of some difficulty, as well as of great importance, both Dr. James and myself wished for a personal interview; and after various proposals of various kinds at length I resolved during the Autumn vacation of 1783 to pay a visit into Cumberland. I thought it would not only amuse my dear wife, but perhaps also be of some use to her health; and I may add, I had also a strong desire once more to see my earliest friends and the land of my nativity. With a view to her health, as well as to our mutual pleasure, I bought a phaeton and a pair of horses, and a saddle-horse for our man-servant, a Yorkshire man, and by far the best manager of horses I have ever known.

Our plan was to go by Lichfield, where we had friends, and to Sir Thomas Broughton's in Staffordshire, whose son was my pupil, and where we were pressed to stay a few days, and by Sandbach, where my Cheshire estate lay, which I wished to see before I sold it. For all this I allowed us a fortnight; and I engaged myself to John James to dine with him in Carlisle on the first Saturday but one after the Monday on which we set out.

Notwithstanding my poor wife's very indifferent state of health, and notwithstanding that I had the ill luck to have bought, I really believe, two of the

worst horses that ever any man drove, my dear
Nelly had such spirits and such an aptness to do
everything as she ought, and George had such skill
respecting horses, that we actually arrived in
Carlisle within a few minutes of the time I had proposed, and in good time for dinner. And that evening we went on to Arthuret.

Here and in its neighbourhood we spent three or
four days; visiting in the meanwhile the Bishop at
Rose Castle, and his son, now Bishop of Killala,
who had married my relation and very good friend
the widow Thomlinson. We then went to Wigton,
and to Blencogo, where I found my poor sister
Tordiff sadly battered by age and disease, but upon
the whole in as good a plight as I could reasonably
expect.

To a person who has never been in a similar situation, it would not be easy to give any tolerably
adequate idea of what I felt on this return to the
place where I was born, and where I had passed
my earliest years. Two and twenty years had gone
over my head since I had even seen the spot, and
thirty since I had lived there. This was a large
portion of the term usually granted to man; and in
my case had been filled up with a vast variety of
events, all of them important to me, on which it
was natural I should now look back and reflect on
with many mingled sensations of regret, satisfaction, hope, and despair. I regretted, as well I
might, that I did not bring back with me the inno-
cence and simplicity with which I left the poor cot-

tage I found much as I had left it; and that its quondam much-honoured tenants were no more, to share with me in the satisfactions my better worldly circumstances might and would have afforded them: I hoped yet to live to make amends for all past errors; but I despaired of her living for whom alone I ardently wished to live.

The people of Blencogo, always uncommonly narrow-minded, came indeed to see me, but it was rather to gaze and to stare than to feel or shew any sincere pleasure on the return of the prodigal. In fact, like the elder brother in the fine parable just alluded to, they seemed rather to envy than to *rejoice with me*. It filled my mind however with a kind of melancholy satisfaction to retrace all the old haunts of my boyish days; and I could and did actually go to every place where anything that had then much interested me had occurred; where I had formerly found a birds' nest I had prized; caught a large trout; fought a successful battle; and above all where my good old father had taken his last leave of me. I knew every field between Blencogo and Bromfield; but when I named their former owners to Isaac, my sister's husband, I seemed to him to be talking of antediluvians. Such changes do but a few years bring about in human affairs. One thing struck me as extraordinary, and even yet I cannot well account for it: every field and every house I went into appeared to me small, and quite disappointed all my notions. Johnson's tavern at Wigton my imagination had long been in the habit of portraying to me as a spacious and respectable house, whereas when I went into it I could scarce find room to swing a cat, and it was with difficulty they convinced me it had not been altered. I had the same ideas as to my own house; and should like to know whether any other person in a similar situation ever felt similar sensations. At Carlisle I looked anxiously and enquired for the King's Arms, where I had formerly been; but I looked and enquired in vain; till some old body or other at length remembered that a great while ago there had been such an inn as I spoke of.

We stayed but three or four days at Blencogo, one of which was a Sunday, when I preached at Bromfield church; and my dearest Nelly rode behind me on our servant's horse, having left our carriage at Wigton. This was the last time she ever heard me preach.

We returned to Arthuret; and after spending one day on the lake of Ulleswater (the only fair day we were favoured with during the fortnight that we were in the county) we set off to return home; which we effected without anything very material occurring to us, excepting that we stopped two or three days with some friends near Rotheram in Yorkshire; and that we travelled as many very agreeably in company with Mr. Mingay, the celebrated lawyer.

I never can look back without astonishment on the spirits and the ability with which my dear wife

performed this journey; which I should have observed I terminated by arriving at Paddington
within five minutes of the time I had proposed
when we left home. She stood even then on the
brink of the grave, and was fully aware of her
danger. She was weak to an extraordinary degree,
frequently sick and in great agony of pain. Yet
she kept up her spirits; attended to everything;
took pleasure in and enjoyed all such incidents as
were at all calculated to give pleasure; and exerted
herself so, that though we frequently set out on our
journeys by five o'clock in the morning, I do not
remember that she ever detained me five minutes.
Her remarks, moreover, were always proper, and
oftentimes highly interesting. Even the poverty
and meanness of Blencogo, and the lowness of my
origin, she saw in their proper light, and spoke of
them in such a manner as could not but greatly
please me. The cordial receptions and the hearty
honest welcomes we everywhere met with, not only
delighted but surprised her. And I still remember
a comparison of hers on the occasion, with which
the Jameses when I told them of it were hardly less
pleased than I was. The people of the north, she
said, were distinguished for the warmth of their
hearts, which she supposed might be owing to their
climate, and effected by some such process in nature as was practised by the people of her country
to make their cider generous and good. It was a
pretty common custom in Virginia and Maryland,
in a cold frosty night, to expose out of doors a

cask of cider, by which means all the aqueous and worthless parts were frozen on the outside, but all the spirit collected in the centre. I must still be permitted to think that there was much real wit and humour, as well as great delicacy and kindness, in this very apt simile.

The few months that this dear and excellent woman lived after our return were literally months of vanity, and a sad succession of wearisome nights and days. She suffered indeed so much, and complained so little; had so little to hope for in this world, and so much in that which is to come, that even I to whom alone her dying could bring misery, at length from mere motives of common humanity seemed almost to wish for the last awful period.

This fatal period did arrive on the night of the 1st of March, 1784. Her poor frame was emaciated and worn down to a skeleton, to such a degree that for several days she could hardly be said to be alive: yet her mind was still vigorous, and her spirits still all alive. She attended to all her domestic concerns, and even ordered dinner, with all her wonted good order; and performed all her devotions, as she had all along done, with unremitting ardour and cheerfulness. But she knew no pulse had been perceptible for some time; and Dr. Smythe, on her earnest importunity, had about two o'clock fairly owned to her he did not think it possible she could continue to hold out through that night. She continued however to sit up; and talked to me as long and as often as her bodily

strength permitted, always sensibly, always af-
fectionately. And she more than once told my
sister, who attended her with the most affectionate
assiduity, that she dreaded the coming hour only
on my account. When the window-shutters were
about to be put to, as the evening was serene and
fine, she said, 'No, not yet, permit me to enjoy the
blessed light of Heaven as long as I can; this may
be my last view of it.' And when about ten o'clock
it was thought necessary she should be put to bed,
John James bade her good night, she fondly took
hold of his hand, and said, 'I seem, I think, now to
be somewhat easier and better, and therefore may
see you again in the morning — if not, be good to
your friend and my dear husband, — and God
bless you!' He could make no reply.

She was got into bed without any apparent
change; and I sat by her to support her head on
account of her difficulty of breathing. In less than
ten minutes she seemed to wake with great agitation from a disturbed doze into which she had
fallen, and then swooned, or as we all thought, died.
She came to again, however, and was able to express her own surprise that it was not death, for she
said her feelings in that moment had been such as
she had never before experienced, and such as it
was impossible we could, any of us, form any just
idea of. She again prayed with infinite fervour
and propriety, both with me and by herself. And
then feeling, I suppose, some such sensations as
she had before experienced, she eagerly and hastily

called out, 'My dear Boucher, if anything can save me, it must be the taking me out of this bed.' I lost not a moment to get her into my arms; when she flung one arm round my neck, and putting her lips to mine, just made shift to say, 'My dear Boucher,' and as I was setting her down on the sofa, breathed her last.

I felt the shock; but falling down on my knees, and in a silent ejaculation calling on God for comfort, I said not a word, nor did I shed a tear. That night I went not into a bed; but next day I was quite composed. And I continued so through all the period of my mourning, with no observable alteration of conduct, excepting that that year I kept the Lent fast with unusual strictness.

I had so long expected, and, as I thought, was so well prepared for this awful event, that I was surprised to find it affect me so much as it did. Conscious that to her it was *of all pain the period, not of joy*, I wept only for myself; for I now found that all my habits of thinking and acting were formed with a view to her; and without her I seemed as if I wanted some of the parts essential to life, a leg, an arm, or an eye. I had so long been accustomed to communicate every thought to her, and to do nothing without first talking the matter over with her, that I seemed actually to have lost the power of thinking or doing anything by myself: and it is a real fact that being under some difficulty as to some orders which it was necessary I should give respecting her funeral, I for a moment so far forgot myself that I went to the door in order to go and consult her. These ideal or imaginary consultations with her are indeed become a part of my settled system of conduct, and not, I trust, without some reason and some advantage. Well as I knew her, and of course can conjecture what in most cases she would think and would say, I am highly sensible that every opinion which I can frame for her must needs be very inferior to what she would have framed for herself. On this point however I am not very anxious to undeceive myself: for, as miserable a substitute as it is, still it is better than acting on my own first crude thoughts; and at any rate it seems to afford me some satisfaction. I endeavour to be as impartial as I can in these imaginary consultations; and I was particularly anxious to be so when I entered on a second marriage; which I still believe I did on such motives and principles as she would have approved of.

In no long time after her death my young friend, Mr. James, went down into the North, and married; and immediately returned to Paddington with his wife; where they sat down in my place. [Seventeen lines crossed out here.]

Some of the boys whom I transferred to them were disorderly and unmanageable. I proposed to the friends of one of the most *obstropolous* of them, the Honble Mr. Ashley, a son of the Earl of Shaftesbury's, an excursion round the Kingdom during the summer's vacation. Such a scheme indeed became absolutely necessary to my own state of mind: and my dear departed angel had foreseen that it would, and recommended it to me. Whilst I stayed at Paddington I could not but feel,

'In every varied posture, place, and hour,
How widowed every thought of every joy':

it was natural therefore that my mind should seek to *wander from its woe*. On my proposing the scheme to the Countess of Shaftesbury, she readily came into it; and greatly improved it by desiring that, excepting my own servant, her son should bear all the expenses of the tour.

Accordingly we set out on horseback, with each of us a servant, early in August. Our first main object was Derbyshire; but we went leisurely through all the intermediate counties, exploring by the way whatever was most curious in each. I made a point of avoiding every place, and in particular every inn, where I had been the preceding year in company so much better and dearer to me. But at Lichfield this happened not to be in my power. I was forced to go to the George Inn there, which is certainly a very good one; and as if that had not been enough, on enquiring about beds, I was told that the only room we could have was one with two beds in it on the first floor. To this I peremptorily objected, but without assigning any reason; and after some altercation the landlord was just going out with orders to get us private lodgings anywhere and at any price, when the chambermaid interposed, and naming me by my name, told

me she was sure I was mistaken,for that the double-
bedded room now offered me was not the one I had
been in the year before. This astonished me; not
only that she could recollect me, but that she had
guessed so well the true cause of my objections, of
which I had not dropped the smallest hint. The
case was, I had been there with my dear Nelly
the preceding year, and in a double-bedded room,
where she had been so ill that I had called up the
maid, and she the mistress, who both thought, as I
did, that she was dying. Her having remembered
this affecting incident, and her supposing that it
now affected me, were certainly extraordinary in
such a character; and prove that sentiment and
even delicacy may be found in all characters. For
if there be any particular classes of mankind that
are particularly unworthy and unamiable in my
eyes, they are hackney-coachmen and postilions,
gentlemen's footmen, and chamber-maids at inns.

After going through all Derbyshire, Manchester,
Liverpool, and Chester, we went into North Wales,
which we entirely traversed, as we also did South
Wales; and from thence proceeded to Saint Giles's
in Dorsetshire, Lord Shaftesbury's seat, where we
terminated our tour. In theory, no doubt, nothing
could be suggested more likely to furnish a person
of an observant turn of mind more satisfaction
than such an expedition: on the trial, however,
I found it far from being pleasant. My companion
was not at all of a congenial temper: the things
that gave me most pleasure gave him none, and

vice versa. I will give one instance of our different tastes, which will shew, better than I could any other way describe it, how little likely it was that his company should be agreeable to me. Going from Conway, we came in sight of the sea, the Isle of Anglesey, Lord Bulkley's fine seat there, Penmaenmawr, all in one moment of time. To heighten the scenery, we happened to be there just as the sun was rising; when the air was remarkably serene and fine, the sea as smooth as glass, and several vessels in sight gliding smoothly over its even surface, with every sail set. It was impossible, I thought, to behold such an assemblage of the finest beauties, unmoved, and I expressed my satisfaction with rapture; on which my companion, with a sang-froid for which I can hardly yet forgive him, wondered what it was that I thought so delightful. He saw indeed water, and stones, and trees, and hills; but for his part he should gaze with far more rapture on a good breakfast. It has been my ill luck thrice to go on very pleasant tours with but unpleasant companions, who could thus analyse the finest buildings and finest prospects into stones, water, trees, and hills, of which all natural beauties must necessarily be combined. In this spirit a French nobleman once commented on the fine prospect from Richmond Hill, which he allowed to be charming, '*mais ôtez*,' said he, '*la rivière et les arbres, &c. et quoi donc!*'

The unsuitableness of my companion was not however the only or most unpleasant circumstance attending this tour. During my absence Mr. and Mrs. James [a line crossed out] resolved to rid themselves, as they hoped, of all farther plague, by getting rid of two of the most obnoxious of their family. Accordingly Mr. Ashley and Mr. Sober (a young man from Barbadoes) were formally expelled. This was a desperate step, and such an one as all my interest and influence could never afterwards wholly retrieve. [Eight lines crossed out.]

Lady Shaftesbury and all her friends resented this measure exceedingly; and whilst I was at Saint Giles's importuned me with such earnestness to finish Mr. Ashley's education, that as they had indeed been brought into their present difficulty chiefly by my means, I hardly knew how to deny them. Mr. Ewer, the young gentleman's guardian, offered me board and accommodation for my servant and a pair of horses, together with two hundred pounds a year, if I would stay with him at Saint Giles's; or four hundred pounds a year if I took him back to my own house at Paddington. These were handsome and tempting offers; and I certainly would have closed with them, could I have done so without seeming to declare myself opposed to my young friends. [Two lines crossed out.]

All such precautions were soon rendered unnecessary by the much-lamented death of the oldest and best friend I had then left in the world, Dr. James, who died on the New Year's Day following. His son was sent for, but did not reach

Arthuret till the good man was no more. It was natural and proper that he should wish to succeed his father in the livings there; which, though held only till a younger son came of age to enter into orders, and was qualified to hold them, were of such value as to render even such a temporary tenure of them a matter of moment. Luckily Sir James Graham, who not long before had come into the possession of the Netherby estate, to which the patronage of these livings belongs, was then in the North, and well disposed towards Mr. James, and so, without waiting for the opinions of some of his more selfish friends, he immediately promised the livings to the son on the same terms that they had been given to the father. And about Lady Day following he left Paddington, and went and settled at Arthuret.

Much about the same time, very unexpectedly, I had an offer of the vicarage of Epsom, which Dr. Glasse, the then incumbent, was disposed to relinquish in my favour. Mr. Parkhurst, the patron, had about three years before given this living to Dr. Glasse; on an idea that if he could not hold it himself, his son, who was just entered into orders, might be glad to have it. Things however took a different turn. Dr. Glasse made interest with the Bishop of London, not only to permit him to resign Hanwell, where he had not only got a new church built, but had also laid out a very large sum of money in repairing the parsonage house, but also to give it to his son; which was accordingly done.

Dr. Glasse moreover, though an exemplarily dis-interested and worthy man, and in as easy and happy circumstances as he wished for, had long, very inconsistently indeed with the rest of his character, been sighing to have some rank and dig-nity in the Church. And so, Mr. Parkhurst, hav-ing, as he apprehended, given him the liberty of nominating his successor to Epsom; and he also having oddly enough persuaded himself that I had some weight and influence with the present Arch-bishop of Canterbury, he wrote to me that if I would employ my interest with the Archbishop to have him made a dignitary, he would nominate me to the vicarage of Epsom. This letter I immedi-ately carried to the Archbishop, who remarked that it was strange it should not have occurred to Dr. Glasse that if I had such interest as he sup-posed, it was natural to imagine I should exert it in my own behalf, and so get the Archbishop to make me a dignitary rather than my friend. His Grace seemed to be hurt also by the notion that I must needs have boasted of my interest with him: and though he really wronged me in thinking so, I have reason to believe the notion has done me material disservice. As however Epsom seemed to be a good situation, and not a bad living, he advised me by all means to accept of it; adding withal that it by no means put it out of the power of my other friends, if they were so disposed, to provide other-wise and better for me.

But when I came to Epsom, and shewed Mr.

Parkhurst Dr. Glasse's letter, he was hardly more astonished than I was. He declared most positively that he had never given away, nor thought of giving away, the appointment to his own living to Dr. Glasse or any other man. Mr. Stevens, through whom alone I well knew I had been thought of, was with me on this occasion, and more affected and hurt than I had ever seen him. However when I had time to recollect myself, I told Mr. Parkhurst that, as he saw I had not been quite a volunteer in this intrusion on him, I hoped he would excuse it, and also feel himself to be as entirely at his own liberty as ever to dispose of his living in any way he should judge proper. He was pleased with this candour and frankness, and so, after handsomely telling me that though he was not personally known to me, he was no stranger to my character, and that therefore had it not been for this strange attempt to wrest from him his own undoubted privilege, there was no man to whom he could with so much satisfaction to his own mind give his living as to myself, he did give it to me then on the condition only that I would reside on it.

Thus was I once more, after an interregnum, as it were, of nine years, a beneficed clergyman. It was not however in my power immediately to remove to my living. The curate was in, and could with no convenience leave the parsonage-house sooner than June: and indeed I should not have chosen to remove my things, and particularly my books, which now exceeded ten thousand volumes, and had cost me upwards of two thousand pounds, in any but a summer month.

Meanwhile Sir Thomas Broughton applied to me to undertake a tour to Germany, to bring home a son of his from thence, and to carry with me a son of Sir Harbord Harbord of Norfolk, now Lord Suffield. These two gentlemen very liberally and handsomely left it to myself to name my own terms for this service, which I did by stipulating only that I should live and travel as a gentleman, and that they should bear my expenses.

On the 20th of June, 1785, in a very complete and elegant travelling-chariot, accompanied by Mr. Harbord and a foreign servant, I set out on this tour. Crossing at Dover, we proceeded through Calais, Saint-Omers, etc., to Brussels; from whence, after staying a week with my friend Lady Eden, she accompanied us in a track-schuit to Antwerp; and from thence we journeyed through Liege, Spa, Aix-la-Chapelle, Düsseldorf, the whole circle almost of Westphalia and Hanover, to Brunswick. Here I stayed upwards of a month; and had the high honour to be much taken notice of at Court, in particular by the Duchess, sister to our King. And indeed in no part of my life, and in no part of the world, did I ever spend my time more entirely to my own satisfaction than I did these few weeks at Brunswick.

Purchasing there of the Honble Charles Fitzroy, son of Lord Southampton, a French travelling-chaise, I set out, along with Mr. Delves Brough-

ton, on my return. We came through Goettingen,
Frankfort, Mannheim, and all along the Rhine, to
Heidelberg and Strasburg; where halting several
days, we went on through Alsace and Lorraine to
Rheims in Champagne, where also we stopped a
few days; and then proceeded to Paris. Here we
stayed a week, and then went to Caen in Normandy, where we spent another week; and finally
obtaining a passage in a merchantman from Havre-
de-Grace on the 5th of October, we landed at Folke-
stone in Kent; and on the 7th got to Sir Thomas
Broughton's house in Mansfield Street, Cavendish
Square, London. Thus in about four months tra-
versing various countries, I travelled not less than
seventeen or eighteen hundred English miles; and
happily performed the difficult errand on which I
was sent, to the entire satisfaction of my employers.
Of this tour I kept an exact journal, as I had done
of that I performed the year before, but which,
sending to my sister in the North by Miss Hodgson,
was most unaccountably lost by their being robbed
of their trunks and portmanteau. My foreign journal is still preserved.

On my return to Epsom, where I seemed now at
length likely to settle for the remainder of my life,
I sat down quietly and steadily to the duties of my
station: my principal amusement being study, and
fitting up my library, now large and valuable.

I found, however, on trial so even and unvaried a
course of life dull, uninteresting, and tiresome, and
not at all suitable to the habits I had now so long

been trained to that they had become a part of my nature. By the advice, and at the request indeed of his Grace the Archbishop of Canterbury, I had resigned my office of Assistant Secretary to the Society; which I had the happiness to do with the testimony of a very general approbation. Yet, excepting this testimony, I have never since received any other marks of the favour of the Society or of any of its leading members; which, to say the least of it, is unusual.

Tired, as has just been hinted, of the insipid insignificance of my present course of life, and bearing in mind also my dearest Nelly's frequent and parting recommendation and advice to me I now began in earnest to turn my thoughts to a second marriage. Aware of a dangerous propensity in my own temper to act from a first impulse, I thought of it long and carefully; and at length on the 10th of August, 1786, without mentioning it to anybody but my sister I wrote a letter on the subject to Miss Foreman of Epsom.

This lady had often been mentioned to me, greatly to her advantage, by my good friend John Frere Esq. as a person every way most suitable to me. She was a maiden lady of about my own age, of most respectable character and a handsome fortune. But being confined much with two sick and elderly maiden aunts, it had never been in my power more than three or four times to be at all in her company, and never once quite alone.

I do not know that I am superstitious; though

being but little afraid of imputations of superstition, made often with very little judgment or reason, I know I am apt to take notice of things that have a superstitious appearance. Something of this sort now occurred respecting Miss Foreman. Being in London, she was for the first time in her life prompted, she knew not why, to go to a woman of the name of Williams, then much celebrated as a fortune-teller. This woman actually told her that she should soon be married, and described me to her in such a way as that it was impossible not to appropriate her description to me: and what is still more extraordinary, she added that the person she was to marry would speak to her next Sunday at the church door. This I actually did; though as far as I was concerned in it, nothing could possibly appear to be more accidental.

On receiving my letter she, agreeably to my request, very soon returned me a very handsome and very proper answer, the purport of which was that, as one of her aunts had died but a few months before, and the other was supposed to be then dying, she could not bring herself then to think of my proposal as her respect for my character made her wish to do. She however immediately apprised her uncle of my intentions; who, for reasons that no doubt appeared to him sufficient, was much against her marrying at all. But he spoke to Mr. Frere, with whom also he was acquainted, and received from him, I presume, such assurances respecting me, as softened at least, though it could not re-

move, his opposition. I was permitted to continue
to write to her; which I did for months very constantly, without its being ever known, or even suspected, that any such thing was in agitation. In
October or November the other aunt died; and, as
soon as with propriety I could, she gave me leave
to visit her; and soon after she paid a visit to some
friends in Saint Alban's, where I followed, and
there stayed a week in the same house with her.
And there all our little difficulties were got over,
and we agreed to be married early in February.

I could have kept the matter a secret to the last:
but as it now seemed unnecessary, on our return
we took no such precautions: and soon after, I took
a large house on Wood-Cote Green, belonging to
Mr. Northey, at one hundred pounds a year; be-
spoke a coach of Mr. Hatchet of Long Acre, which
cost me very near two hundred pounds; hired servants, and bought plate, china, etc. The settlement too was made. Her fortune was nearly
fourteen thousand pounds, which it was agreed
should be laid out in the funds, and be made up
twenty thousand pounds stock, out of my money,
to be settled on her for ever if she survived me, but
to be mine for my life if I survived her; and after
my decease, to be at her disposal by will. The
trustees were Charles Foreman Esq. who was her
uncle, John Frere Esq. and William Mount Esq.

But before I go on any further with my narrative, it may not be unnecessary to give a more particular account or description of the person who is

now hereafter to bear so near and great a part in my history. She was a native of Angmoring, near Arundel, in Sussex; but had been brought up almost from her infancy [by] and had resided almost altogether with, her grandmother and aunts here at Epsom. Her person was rather beneath the middle size, and somewhat embonpoint: but though she was not of an elegant make, she had a fine and dignified presence, and pleasing features, with a brunette and ruddyish complexion. Her teeth were good, and her eye animated and sparkling: and of all the men and women I ever heard in my life her voice, I think, was the sweetest. Of her temper and character I may speak hereafter with more propriety.

On the 15th February, 1787, we were married in the church of Saint Michael in Saint Alban's by her friend the Revd. Mr. Gape, attended by her elder uncle, Mr. Luke Foreman, heretofore a Lisbon merchant, and her bosom friend Mrs. Alexander; and came back on the same day with Mrs. Alexander and Miss Mary Fothergill to our own house here on Woodcote Green. And here we set out pleasantly and with fair and happy prospects, though on an expensive establishment, viz. four horses and seven servants; with a large and genteel acquaintance in a genteel but dear neighbourhood. For the two or three first months we were seldom without company; though it was a state of life that by no means afforded me any adequate gratifications; yet as I possessed many other great and substantial blessings, I was resolved not to suffer one or two unpleasant circumstances to disturb my happiness.

By some means or other I have omitted to mention in its place that in August, 1784, my brother-in-law, Mr. Carr of Maryland had sent over to me for their education the three eldest sons of my Nelly's deceased eldest brother, whose widow had married again not very prudently; and Mr. Carr had become the guardian of these children and their estate in my place. At first I put them under the care of Mr. James; but on his leaving that line of life I sent them to Deptford, under Mr. Lewis who had heretofore been my assistant. Mr. Lewis was engaged in an academy there, in connexion with a Mr. Hutton, a deep and not very good man, who was too many for Mr. Lewis; and accordingly after a long series of most disagreeable wrangling Lewis left the place; and I removed my nephews, placing them then with my own curate here, Mr. Golding, and boarding them with my sister in the Vicarage. And this scheme so well intended added prodigiously to my other enormous expenses; for remittances came over very slow and very scanty. At this moment (September 18th, 1788) they must needs owe me upwards of six hundred pounds, which, were it all paid, would leave me a loser by the experiment.

During this spring also I had the misfortune to lose another nephew, the only son of my sister Tordiff, whom I had a year or two before placed at

Appleby school, with an intention of giving him at least a good education, if I did not also make him my heir. He was a fine youth, of good parts, a sweet temper, and amiable manners, dying in his eleventh year. I felt his loss exceedingly.

This great loss, however, seemed soon after to be much and happily mitigated by my dear wife's being declared to be with child. As she was then nearly fifty years of age I was almost afraid to believe what I so much wished: however, so many circumstances concurred to give it credibility, that for many months I was fully persuaded of it. Mrs. Alexander and Mrs. Chandler, her most intimate and confidential friends, and who had both of them had several children, both believed it to be so; and so did not only Mrs. Lambe, but a Mrs. Lazonby, an eminent accoucheur from Chelsea, who attended her two or three times on the occasion.

Full of this idea, in June we made a visit to her brother, Mr. John Foreman, at Angmoring, and stayed with him three months. And all the time she regularly increased in size; was sick almost constantly, and everything seemed to go on just as might have been expected. Angmoring is a charmingly neat and orderly village in a charming country. Mr. Foreman has a fine farm called Egglesden just at the end of it. The house is large, old, and venerable, being supposed to be the remains of some monastery. The sea is distant about a mile or two, and in full view. Near it also is High Down Hill, which is absolutely one of the finest spots of

earth I ever saw, for it has everything that can
recommend any place. Mr. Foreman is an hospitable, affectionate, kind-hearted man as ever
lived; and I did enjoy much real pleasure while I
was there, and should much more had my mind
been quite at ease respecting my poor wife, who
still suffered much, though as we hoped in a good
cause.

Whilst I was on this visit I received the first
dividend of the compensation allotted by Government to American Loyalists. My present allotment was nine hundred pounds. Mr. James
Brooks, a very obliging, useful man, whom I had
long known both abroad and at home, being left
very destitute by means of the rebellion, was com-
mendably exerting himself to earn a little to support himself, an aged mother, and a deformed aunt,
by doing something in the wine trade. But he had
no capital: I lent him two hundred and fifty pounds
of this money to begin with; and with most of the
rest I bought thirty pounds a year in the Long Annuities for my sister. I had also this year paid off
to Mr. W. Lyon a Bond I had long ago given him
for a thousand pounds, payable at my death: to do
this I sold out fifty pounds in the Long Annuities,
having before sold out a hundred pounds a year to
enable me to complete my wife's settlement. Mr.
Lyon is either to replace twenty pounds in the
Long Annuities, or to give his bond for the payment of twenty pounds a year, till it is so replaced,
to my sister; so that she now has, as I have long

wished her to have, fifty pounds a year, independent of me.

Woes cluster says Young, and so do lesser grievances; for as though the infinite sluices of expense that had now all at once been opened for the expenditure of my little fortune, which, abundant as, comparing it with anything I had been used to suppose it possible for me ever to attain, it certainly was, yet was not equal to all these endless drains: I say, as if all these had been too few, Mr. Harford, the natural son of Lord Baltimore, to whom in an evil hour I had become security for the late Sir Robert Eden in a Bond for twelve hundred pounds, now called upon me for payment of principal and interest, amounting in all to fifteen hundred pounds. After infinite difficulty and vexation I at length borrowed of a Mr. Pagett of Warwickshire a thousand pounds, which Mr. Harford was graciously pleased to accept of in lieu of the whole. Mrs. James (who by the death of my amiable and very dear young friend was now become an amiable and dear widow) happening since to have a thousand pounds to lend out, I have borrowed that sum of her on bond at 4½ per cent. and have repaid Mr. Pagett. This was a heavy blow, and it fell on me, if not unpitied, yet certainly unassisted, by all the Eden family, great and powerful as they all are.

All these disasters, however, were nothing to the dreadful disappointment and calamity which now hung over me, suspended only by a thread, and which soon overtook me. My poor wife after our return daily grew worse and worse, and I of course more and more anxious and uneasy. Mrs. Lazonby was again consulted, and was again confident of pregnancy: nor, notwithstanding the anasarcous swellings which had so alarmed me, did Mr. Lambe begin to doubt till after Christmas. Early in January my good friend Dr. Carmichael Smyth was sent for to Epsom, and regularly consulted. At first even he doubted; but before he left us he pronounced there was some visceral disease, though he could not then well say what, but he thought it was an enlarged ovarium; and in short he told me in confidence he feared the case was a bad one. As, however, sundry hydropsical symptoms now appeared manifest, and the idea of pregnancy now given up, medicines were regularly administered for the dropsy, but with little or no success.

It is impossible to describe how much I felt my disappointment: to have children had been the fond object of my fondest wishes all my life; and after I had so long counted with such confidence on having one, the disappointment alone would have been more than I could well bear, even if it had not been attended with prospects for the future still more alarming. Yet I am not sure whether I do not owe to those very prospects my having been able to bear up under my great disappointment so well as I did; having often observed that great evils render us insensible of lesser ones.

Too well convinced as I was of the serious

amount of her maladies, I found little difficulty to prevail on her to go to London (where however she had often said she never could live) to be near the ablest medical assistance. Early in March we went: took lodgings in Great Marlborough Street; and there for full three months she was almost daily visited by Dr. Smyth, Sir George Baker, Mr. Howard the surgeon, and Mr. Fowle the apothecary. Their endeavours were directed chiefly against the dropsy: and though there certainly was no proof that it was at all owing to their medicines, she was at length, and almost all at once, much relieved, if not cured, of the dropsy. Some ugly symptoms still stuck by her; yet I could not help cherishing some hopes that by the blessing of God she might once more be restored to health and to me: nor, though they were less sanguine, were her physicians now, I believe, wholly without hopes. As the principal object of attention now seemed to be the bracing again the slackened system and recovering strength, they urged us to return to the country; as we did. And from that time to last Sunday she has very slowly indeed, but far too surely, gradually been growing worse. Her case seemed to become what used to be called an atrophy: she gradually lost her appetite and her strength, and was also in constant danger of a general mortification, to which there was a constant tendency. One thing in the progress of her disease seemed remarkable to me; it advanced not steadily and regularly, but as it were by fits and starts. As for instance: after a day and a night, or perhaps two, very bad and very alarming, she got better, and continued better for a week or fortnight, when she probably had another bad fit, every one of which though she seemed to recover from left her essentially weaker and worse. For many months she was not able to stir or move, but as she was lifted and helped; nor did I ever see any creature so reduced, and so mere a skeleton: for more than a month the back-bone had come through the skin, and towards the close that was the case almost all over her frame, and there was no whole part about her. At length after being more dead than alive for above a week, on Sunday the 14th inst. appearing to be in the agonies of death for five or six hours, about five o'clock in the evening she was released from all her sufferings, and left me once more a poor, helpless, forlorn individual.

Something should now be said of her character, which though I probably understood better than any other person, yet as it appeared to me to be (like characters in general) a mixed one, and I am very desirous to be impartial, I feel it not to be easy in the present state of my mind to proceed.

What I have seen of her has convinced me still more than ever that mankind in general are just what education makes them. Naturally she was one of the loveliest and dearest of women; yet somehow or other she had picked up some notions and habits, which were less amiable, or (as perhaps I should rather have said) less suitable to my notions and habits. Her temper was even, her manners almost beyond example gentle and mild, and all her affections and passions without blame. She never, that I know of, gave offence; yet though she was always regarded as a respectable woman, I have thought she sometimes failed to please, and even by her friends seemed to be more esteemed than loved. All this, as has just been hinted, was clearly owing to her education. She had from her infancy been taught to consider herself as one of the first fortunes of her day, and had learned to place an undue reliance on great wealth, as though it had been a thing of indifference whether a person possessed of wealth possessed anything else or not. This produced an habitual unconcern about the opinions of others in matters of slight moment; and so when she failed to please it seemed to be because she took no pains to please. She had too been habituated to be gratified in every personal indulgence to an extraordinary degree, and so could bear no pain. I never saw a person of so much good sense and good temper submit to sickness and sorrow with so very ill a grace. She seemed indeed to have no fortitude; nor (as it is in the nature of such habits of indulgence to render those who give way to them eminently selfish) did she frequently recollect or regard what pain she gave others, so she could but gain, or fancy she gained, a little ease to herself. To a mind endowed with sensibility nothing can possibly give greater pain than the seeing a beloved object suffer, without being able to mitigate those sufferings. She seemed not to think of this; for though, as she might have seen, her moanings and screams wrung every fibre of my heart, she never was awake a minute whilst she had strength without moaning and screaming, even whilst we who stood by her had no proofs that her pains were intense. Even to this moment those heart-piercing moans of hers seem to be vibrating on my ears. But her greatest defect in my eye was, that her mind was very faintly imbued with a sense of religion. Yet she was really and substantially a good woman, and had no foul and unsubdued passions. She was not however without religion, both internal and external: all I mean is, it did not seem to have laid such fast hold, nor to have made so strong an impression, on such a mind as hers was, as, if she had been differently brought up, it certainly would. In her conduct no person was ever more blameless; and she took much pleasure in doing good; but it seemed to proceed rather from a natural goodness of heart than from religious motives.

Her lesser faults were, she had been suffered to contract habits of indolence: I never saw any person sleep so much and stir so little. She was fond also of magnificence and splendour: and though we certainly had fortune and income enough to have satisfied all our reasonable desires, yet having with good reason expected a much larger fortune than she got, she felt more pain from what she was disappointed of than pleasure in what she had. Her

uncle having, apparently at least, preferred some
distant (and, as she thought, less worthy) relations
to her, was the source of infinite and perpetual
uneasiness to her, and embittered, if it did not
shorten her life.

With all these drawbacks she was an excellent
and amiable woman; and I now find I loved her
more cordially than as long as she lived I was aware
of. Had it pleased God to have spared her life, I
have not a doubt but that she would have been, in
the utmost meaning of the words, a good wife; as I
bless God, excepting her sad sicknesses, she really
was, and often said she was a happy one. She had
no wayward humours to conquer, no egregious follies, and not a single vice; and had a thousand
merits and virtues. Her attachment to me moreover was ardent and sincere; and this she mani-
fested by every word and deed to the latest moment of her life. It is indeed substantially mani-
fested by her having made no Will; by which means
I now come in for the whole of her fortune: for
which, as well as for ten thousand other endearing
circumstances I hope God will give me grace always
to love and honour her memory. *Vale, mea Maria,
conjux dilectissima, vale!*

What I shall now do, or how or where I shall
hereafter dispose of myself, I am totally at a loss to
conjecture. In a few days after her funeral I am
now proposing once more to set out on a scheme of
wandering; and am going to the North to make in
the first place a sort of an experiment on myself,

whether, with all the habits I have now acquired, I could again bear to live there, as I am so often disposed to fancy I can. I have now greatly added to my Blencogo estate, which Tordiff supposes would sell for two thousand guineas or more, and let for eighty pounds a year. If I find any amusement or pleasure, as I hope I shall, in farming, and in improving of an estate (an idea now almost always uppermost in my thoughts) my intentions are to make, if I can with propriety and advantage, a considerable purchase. But at any rate I hope to return to Epsom before Christmas, and am willing to believe that whilst I do live I shall live more at Epsom than any place else.

10th March 1789

I stayed in the North nearly three months; and upon the whole found far more resources and amusement than, before I had tried it, I had dared to flatter myself with the hopes of. Among other things, I added two or three fresh purchases to my estate at Blencogo; made some exchanges with Mr. Thomlinson, and also enfranchised it. I now also in earnest took measures for building; and accordingly orders are given, and already carrying into execution, for a very complete farmhouse, with all necessary outhouses and offices. The whole, it is estimated, will cost about five hundred pounds.

During my stay in Cumberland, after looking at sundry estates on sale, and trying to treat for them, I at length bought one called Lang-Holm-Row of

Mr. John Simpson of Sebergham. This estate is singularly compact and convenient, containing a hundred and twelve acres, the greatest part of which is freehold, and extends upwards of a mile westwards from the river Caldew, which is its eastern boundary. The purchase-money was two thousand guineas; and I thought it to the credit both of Mr. Simpson and myself, that this sum was the first and only offer I made.

Having paid two visits to my good friends the Jameses at Longtown, by their advice and assistance, I placed my two nieces under the care of a Mrs. Holden at Carlisle; in the hope that they would not only unlearn some vulgar and perhaps dangerous notions and habits acquired at Blencogo, but also in some degree acquire, if not a liberality, yet a decency, of manners. I propose that they shall remain with Mrs. Holden about half a year.

Early in December I returned to my melancholy and uncomfortable home here at the Vicarage; having been called back somewhat sooner than perhaps I should have wished by some disagreeable difficulties that had occurred respecting my claims on Government as an American Loyalist. In the hope, as it would seem, of recovering something from the wreck of my confiscated property in Maryland, my well-meaning but (in this instance at least) ill-judging friends in America had sought for and made out, on almost any pretence, sundry debts which it was to be supposed I owed there, to an amount of two thousand pounds sterling. These imaginary debts, when presented to the Congress Commissioners, were (as might easily have been foreseen) disallowed, because no doubt they could not be authenticated either upon oath or by any legal proofs. But though disallowed in Maryland, the Congressionalists there were too liberal-minded and too public-spirited wholly to disregard them: they were sent home to the Commissioners appointed by Parliament here, clearly with an intention of prejudicing my claims on this Government. After various applications, memorials, and examinations, I have, however, at length got these untoward and very unpleasant claims settled; and having received nine hundred pounds last year, my final allotment is now fixed at eighteen hundred and fifty pounds more, which I hope to receive, with some discount, in the course of the present year. Besides this, an allowance or pension of one hundred and twenty pounds per annum is settled on me for life, as a compensation for the loss of my Preferment.

Finding again now on a second trial the Vicarage house extremely inconvenient, and quite too small, particularly for my books, and also impossible to be enlarged and improved at any reasonable expense, soon after Christmas I was induced to purchase of Richard Sheldon Esq. of Lincoln's Inn, a very good house, with about five acres of land, all freehold, on Clay-Hill. The price was one thousand and twenty-five pounds, which is now paid, and the premises all regularly conveyed to me. There are but two material objections to this house; it is too far distant from the church, and Clay-Hill is a bad place for water. This house also wanted some repairs, and, as might have been expected in any house I could have bought, it wanted a good room or two for my books. These I am now going to supply, having just entered into a contract with B. Gavdom, a workman of this town, under the direction of Mr. Gwilt, a Surveyor in the borough, to make many specified alterations and additions for three hundred and ninety pounds. The whole, exclusive of furniture, it may be expected will stand me in not less than fifteen hundred pounds. It is all to be finished by July.

I have also, since I left the North, added still more to my Blencogo estate by the purchase of three fields of Miss Robinson for one hundred pounds; and of sundry fields, etc. of William Barnes of The Beck for three hundred and forty pounds.

END OF THE AUTOBIOGRAPHY

Mr. Boucher married (for the third time) Mrs. James, the 'amiable and dear widow' mentioned in his narrative, by whom he had eight children. He died at Epsom on the 27th April, 1804.

Copy of memorial tablet in Bromfield Church, near Wigton, Cumberland

In memory of James Boucher of a family of yeomanry settled at Blencogo on the same estate for many generations.

Having resided several years in Dublin, he there acquired a great urbanity of manners, and being also a pleasant, sensible and worthy man, he was highly esteemed by a numerous and respectable acquaintance, and much endeared to his family.

He was born at Blencogo on the 1st of January, 1694, and died at the same place on the 14th December, 1768.

Also of Ann, the daughter of Thomas and Jane Barnes of Little Bampton in this County, and wife of the above-named James Boucher. She was a woman of exemplary industry, frugality, and piety, and was very careful to bring up her children (of whom four lived and arrived at maturity of years) in the nurture and admonition of the Lord. She was born on the 1st of March 1704, and died on the 19th November, 1765.

Also of John their eldest son, who, being in Holy Orders, was at the time of his death settled at Wickham near Newcastle-upon-Tyne, as Curate of that large and populous parish. At that place he married Alice Dawson, a well-educated woman of a respectable family and connexions in Manchester. Dying very soon after his marriage, he left only one posthumous daughter; and neither his widow nor his child survived him long. He was a studious man and a good scholar; conscientious and careful in the performance of his public duties, he was much regarded as a good parish priest, and not less regarded for the gentleness of his manners and the extraordinary benevolence and sweetness of his temper. He was born at Blencogo on the 19th of September, 1734, and died at Wickham on the 10th of June, 1765; and in the church at Wickham there is a plain slab monument that covers his remains and records his name.

Also of Jane Boucher, their youngest daughter, who, when her younger brother went to North America, followed his fortunes, and resided with him in Virginia and Maryland several years. A truer friend was never known. After passing a large portion of her life abroad, towards the close of it she had the happiness to return, and retire to the place of her nativity; and there, after a life of great trials and troubles, like the perfect man mentioned by the Psalmist, her end was peace. She was born at Blencogo on the 2nd of February, 1742, and died there on the 13th of April, 1794.

Also in memory of JONATHAN, son of the above, born at Blencogo, 1738, died at Epsom, 1804. He for many years lived in America, till he at length became the victim of those troubles, which with unshaken loyalty, integrity, and zeal, he vainly endeavoured to stem. He returned to his native country, poor in all things but the riches of a blameless conscience. He was nineteen years Vicar of Epsom in Surrey, and died regretted by the poor, the learned, and the good.

And also of their daughter Mary, who departed this life on the 16th of April, 1823, in the eighty-seventh year of her age, and who was twenty-two years the wife, and three years the widow, of Isaac Tordiff, of Blencogo.

All the above left their surviving relatives and friends here in happy hopes of their joyful resurrection to eternal life hereafter.

Also in memory of Elizabeth, wife of the above Reverend Jonathan Boucher, who died on the 12th of October, 1846, at Seagrave Rectory, Leicestershire, in the eighty-fifth year of her age.

The following inscription was placed on a monument in Epsom church:

Near this place are deposited, in the hope of a blessed

resurrection to eternal life, the remains of the Reverend Jonathan Boucher, M.A., F.A.S., nineteen years Vicar of this parish: He was born at Blencogo in Cumberland 12th March, 1738, and died 27th April, 1804.

A faithful steward of the mysteries of God, he ever maintained and enforced, both by his writings and discourses, that form of sound doctrine delivered unto the Saints; whilst in his opinions and practice he exhibited a bright example of Christian charity.

Few men possessed a larger store of various knowledge, or greater liberality of communication; and the success with which, in the intervals of more important pursuits, he cultivated English Philological Antiquities, will excite the regret of all the learned for the event, which has left his valuable labours unfinished.

His loyalty to his King remained unshaken, even when the madness of the people raged furiously against him; and, for conscience sake, he resigned ease and affluence in America, to endure hardships and poverty in his native land; but the Lord gave him twice as much as he had before, and blessed his latter end more than his beginning.

THE END